Telling
Yourself
the
Truth

Books by Dr. William Backus

The Good News About Worry
The Healing Power of a Christian Mind
Learning to Tell Myself the Truth
Telling Each Other the Truth
Telling the Truth to Troubled People
Telling Yourself the Truth*
What Your Counselor Never Told You

*with Marie Chapian

Telling Yourself the Truth

WILLIAM BACKUS
AND MARIE CHAPIAN

BETHANY HOUSE PUBLISHERS
a division of Baker Publishing Group
Minneapolis, Minnesota

Published by Bethany House Publishers
11400 Hampshire Avenue South
Bloomington, Minnesota 55438
www.bethanyhouse.com

Bethany House Publishers is a division of
Baker Publishing Group, Grand Rapids, Michigan

Printed in the United States of America

Library of Congress Cataloging-in-Publication Data
Backus, William D.
     Telling yourself the truth : find your way out of depression, anxiety, fear, anger, and other common problems by applying the principles of misbelief therapy / William Backus and Marie Chapian.
        pages cm
     Includes bibliographical references.
     Summary: "This perennially popular book continues to help people find their way out of depression, anxiety, fear, anger, and other common problems. Includes a study guide"— Provided by publisher.
     ISBN 978-0-7642-1193-5 (pbk. : alk. paper)
     1. Christian life. 2. Happiness. I. Chapian, Marie. II. Title.
     BV4501.3.B33 2014
     248.4—dc23   2013039377

Cover design by Eric Walljasper

22   23   24   25   12   11   10   9   8

In keeping with biblical principles of creation stewardship, Baker Publishing Group advocates the responsible use of our natural resources. As a member of the Green Press Initiative, our company uses recycled paper when possible. The text paper of this book is composed in part of post-consumer waste.

Contents

Contents

Introduction

This book has been written to help you live with the one person you must live with for life—you. The precepts set forth here are not new; in fact, they've been around since the time of King Solomon and before. People become happy and contented by learning how to practice the habits this book describes.

The current writings of the cognitive therapists such as Albert Ellis, A. T. Beck, M. J. Mahoney, D. Meichenbaum and Arnold Lazarus and their scientific points of view, the writings of philosophers such as Titus and Marcus Aurelius, the findings of psychological researchers as well as the probings of the greatest minds of history bring us to the truths set forth in the Holy Scriptures and the principles we share here with you. These principles are so practical and time-tested—in fact, God's own method for destroying the strongholds of evil in the minds of men and women—that it is amazing the average reader has never heard of such things!

Most of us want to be honest-to-goodness happy human beings who can handle life well and manage to feel good in spite of ever-increasing odds against us. Ironically, we use methods of achieving happiness that make us *unhappy*. We work at and strive for something that we can't quite catch hold of.

What does it mean to be happy? We could define it as a continuing sense of well-being, a state of feeling good about life, others, and self. We could also define happiness as the absence of mental and emotional discomfort and pain. The Bible calls happy "blessed."

> Blessed—*happy*, fortunate, prosperous and enviable—is the man who walks and lives not in the counsel of the ungodly. . . . But his delight and desire are in the law of the Lord, and on His law—the precepts, the instructions, the teachings of God—.[1]

In the Sermon on the Mount, Jesus names those who are blessed, or happy. They are people who are "spiritually prosperous [that is, with life-joy and satisfaction in God's favor and salvation, regardless of their outward conditions]."[2]

What is your definition of happiness? After you answer that question, we want you to know that it's possible to be happy, really happy in the deepest corners of your being, and to stay that way. You don't have to be a victim of circumstances, events, relationships. You don't have to be trapped by persistent painful emotions.

This book is written to help you possess the happiness you desire and to be the person you'd like to be. You can live happily ever after with the person you are and make a profound affect on those around you because of it.

"Misbelief Therapy," as we have called our *modus operandi,* involves putting the truth into our value systems, philosophies, demands, expectations, moralistic and emotional assumptions, as well as into the words we tell ourselves. The Bible says it is the *truth* that sets man free. Jesus Christ is the living Truth. When we inject the truth into our every thought, taking a therapeutic broom

1. Psalm 1:1, 2.
2. Matthew 5:3.

8

and sweeping away the lies and misbeliefs which have enslaved us, we find our lives radically changed for the happier better.

It is our hope that other professionals will join us in the exciting discovery that truth as it is in Jesus is a teachable way of life which leads to wholeness, restored functioning, and freedom from neurosis.

We ask the indulgence of our professionally trained readers who will find little scientific terminology in this book. We have purposely eschewed "psychologese" in order that all of our readers will feel comfortable with us.

Recently we completed a research project which involved follow-up calls to every client seen at the Center for Christian Psychological Services in a six-month period. The purpose was to ascertain how well Misbelief Therapy, as we call it, had actually worked in the lives of the clients. The results were gratifying. Ninety-five percent of the clients that had been treated at the Center had improved. Not only that, but these people were able to cite specific behaviors which had changed for the better. They were enthusiastic over the treatment they had received and the results that had been obtained in their lives. That is why we feel confident in recommending that you not only read this book, but that you also put into practice the procedures it offers you for bringing about real change in your life. You will be learning skills which you will want to keep forever.

What Is Misbelief?

"Why do I feel the way I do?" cries the troubled person. Typically, he or she wants to put the blame on something or someone else. "It's my wife. *She's* the one who makes me feel this way." Or, "It's all my *husband's* fault." "My job isn't satisfying me," or *"My friends* are disappointing," or "My *children* are a disappointment." Some people blame their problems on their church. They find fault with their pastor, complain that the people aren't friendly enough or that everybody *else* in the world is a hypocrite.

There's something in all of our lives we'd like to change. No-body's life circumstances are perfect. But what are we *telling* ourselves about these circumstances?

A few years ago a man we'll call Jerry was a wreck of a man. He was a Christian and had believed in God most of his life. Now, however, after 15 years of marriage, he was forced to live alone, separated from his family and facing a divorce he didn't want. He thought it was the end of the world. He was really miserable. He spent many evenings trying to anesthetize his painful feelings with liquor. He was so unhappy he wanted to die because he just couldn't see any other way out of such sad circumstances.

Finally, he decided to see a Christian psychotherapist for help. Once in therapy, he gradually began to see that his life didn't have to be over. He stopped thinking about taking his own life, and his faith in God began to stretch. He started thinking of God as a giver of *good*. He came to know Him in a new dimension, and little by little, his life changed.

He explained it this way. "One day while I sat groveling in my sorrows, I listened to the words I had been telling myself, things like, 'Oh, what's the use? I'm all alone. Nobody loves me or cares about me. Nobody wants to be with me. I'm rejected and useless . . . ' Suddenly I was shocked. I thought, 'What am I telling myself anyhow?' "

Jerry questioned his self-talk. He recognized something radically wrong with what he had been telling himself and realized his depression was not due to his impending divorce, but what he was *telling himself about it.*

As a result he began to change the sentences he said to himself. This took some hard work and determination on his part. It wasn't easy at first, but because he refused to be a "chump" to a pack of self-destroying lies, he taught himself to confess the truth.

INSTEAD OF:	HE SAID:
I'm a failure and no good.	The marriage failed, but I am deeply loved by God. Therefore I am important.
I'm so lonely and miserable.	I'm alone, but I am not lonely.
I'm separated from my family and there's no joy anymore for me.	I'm separated from my family and that hurts. I can function even though I hurt.

He also stopped drinking completely. He argued with the destructive sentences he had been telling himself. "Just because I'm alone doesn't mean I have to be lonely!" he said. He told himself the *truth* and used his situation as an opportunity to celebrate, enjoy and revel in the presence of the Lord Jesus Christ in his life.

His circumstances hadn't changed, but what he *told himself* about the circumstances changed! He discovered that he had been telling himself a lot of lies, straight from the devil.

Three steps to becoming the happy person you were meant to be are:

1. *Locate your misbeliefs.* (Jerry realized that he was telling himself lies.)
2. *Remove them.* (He argued against them. "I am *not* lonely!")
3. *Replace misbeliefs with the truth.* ("It's nonsense to say I'm unlovable and useless. I'm loved with an everlasting love by the God of the universe. In Him, I have countless talents and uses and I am infinitely valuable to Him.")

Jerry learned that being alone could actually be an exciting experience with the Lord. If he had hung on to his ridiculous misbeliefs, he might have gone to his grave in gloom and misery long ago. Happily, he recovered completely and now leads a wonderfully fulfilled life. He will never again suffer the self-destructive anguish he was duped by once. When he learned to see the *truth* about himself, he also learned to argue and get rid of the lies that would have destroyed him.

Truth: What Is It?

Many philosophers and thinkers through the ages have been fascinated by the idea of *truth,* what it is and what it means in our lives.

One of these people was a man named Rene Descartes. He was a devout Roman Catholic who lived at the beginning of the seventeenth century. He made a name for himself by trying to discover clear and indubitable truth.

Descartes was fed up with the never-ending arguments among philosophers and decided to put an end to their disagreements forever.

In order to find some truth which would be so unquestionable that no one could doubt it, Descartes decided to start at the point of his own doubt of things. He systematically doubted all that he could possibly doubt. In doubting everything imaginable, he told himself he was *thinking*. Then he reasoned, since he was thinking, he had to *be*.

Thus emerged his famous words, "*I think, therefore I am.*" Descartes had finally discovered what he considered an indubitable truth: He believed the most important thing about truth was to arrive at it. The trouble with his proposition is that it doesn't tell us much about how to *live* or be *happy* with that truth.

Marcus Aurelius was another thinking man. He was emperor of Rome about 150 years after Christ, and he too was concerned with the *truth*. Marcus Aurelius was a stoic ruler and noted as one of the most high-minded and conscientious of all the Roman emperors. He had many failings, one of them his dislike for Christians; but in spite of this sorrowful indiscretion, he pursued a quest for *truth*. In his book *Meditations*, he shares an earth-shaking discovery, one that can make a difference in the way we live today.

Marcus Aurelius saw that human emotion is not just a product of chance circumstances, but is determined by the way people *think*.

Where Descartes said, "I think, therefore I am," Marcus Aurelius might have said, "I think in order to *determine* the way I am."

Precisely.

In the book of Proverbs in the Bible, it reads, *As a man thinketh in his heart, so is he.*[1] In exploring this and other scriptural references pertaining to the importance of right thinking, we discover the Bible solidly teaches that man's feelings, passions and behavior are subject to and conditioned by the way he thinks.

1. Proverbs 23:7.

Marcus Aurelius had unearthed a truth whose fullness he could not wholly appreciate because he did not know the Lord Jesus Christ who said, "*I am the Truth.*"[2]

As human beings we are not doomed to a cold, emotionless, machine-like existence. We are creatures throbbing with mental, emotional and physical energy. Once we yank out the irrationalities and lies from our thoughts and replace them with the *truth*, we can lead satisfying, rich and fulfilling emotional lives.

These irrationalities are not always easy to label. Most of what we tell ourselves is not in word form. Our thoughts are often images or attitudes without words attached to them. You may feel uncomfortable and isolated in crowded places but never actually put these feelings into words. You may be fearful of a thing and avoid it without really knowing what's going on in your belief system at all.

But how do we change? How do we make contact with what's really going on within us?

"Doctor," a patient will weep, "I think the root of my problem goes back to my childhood!" How often we hear this statement!

Our culture, intinctured with Freudian philosophy, has nearly made it mandatory to believe that no one can be healed psychologically without exploring the past in detail and in depth.

It is not, however, events either past or present which make us feel the way we feel, but our *interpretation of those events.*

Our feelings are not caused by the circumstances of our long-lost childhood *or* the circumstances of the present. *Our feelings are caused by what we tell ourselves about our circumstances,* whether in words or in attitudes.

What we tell ourselves can be either (1) truth or (2) lie.

If you tell yourself untruths or lies, you will *believe* untruths and lies. If you tell yourself you're a dumb jerk who can't do anything

2. "I am the Way and the Truth and the Life; no one comes to the Father except by (through) Me" (John 14:6).

right, you'll believe it. If you *believe* something, you'll *act* as though you believe it.

That's why your *beliefs and misbeliefs* are the most important factors of your mental and emotional life.

Misbeliefs

What are misbeliefs?

The word *misbelief* is an important word. In fact, it's the most appropriate label we can think of for some of the ridiculous things we tell ourselves. The amount of suffering we experience due to sustained bouts of negative thinking and battered emotions is outrageous.

Misbeliefs are the direct cause of emotional turmoil, maladaptive behavior and most so-called "mental illness." Misbeliefs are the cause of the destructive behavior people persist in engaging in even when they are fully aware that it is harmful to them (such as overeating, smoking, lying, drunkenness, stealing or adultery).

Misbeliefs generally appear as truth to the person repeating them to himself. They might even seem to be true to an untrained counselor. That is partly because they often do contain some shred of truth, and partly because the sufferer has never examined or questioned these erroneous assumptions. But, please understand, the misbeliefs we tell ourselves are directly from the pit of hell. They are hand engraved and delivered by the devil himself. He is very clever in dishing out misbeliefs. He doesn't want to risk being discovered so he always appears as if the lie he is telling us is true.

Words like, "Oh, I can't do anything right. I'm always making mistakes" are good examples. You'll believe these lies when you've just made a mistake.

"Oh, I can't do anything right" is a *misbelief statement*. If you believe words like that, you are believing a lie.

Martin Luther, teaching the meaning of the sixth petition of the Lord's Prayer ("Lead us not into temptation") wrote: "We pray in this petition that God would guard and keep us lest the devil, the world, and our flesh lead us into misbelief, despair and other great shame and vice." The consequences of misbelief do lead to despair and other "great shame and vice."

Think for a moment about the things you tell yourself. If you tell yourself your mother-in-law hates you or the guy next door is a rotten neighbor and a no-good so-and-so, what will you be influenced by? *You'll believe what you tell yourself.* Therefore, you'll treat your mother-in-law as a personal enemy and you'll treat your neighbor exactly like a no-good so-and-so.

More than likely your mother-in-law and neighbor gave you some reason to tell yourself those things about them, so you can feel justified with your self-talk. But you're a victim of misbelief.

Why?

The Apostle James shows us where destructive self-talk comes from. "This [superficial] wisdom is not such as comes down from above, but is earthly, unspiritual [animal], even devilish."[3] Negative and distorted statements which a person repeats to himself come from the devil. Your flesh accepts them without question and then, like spoiled, rotting food, these words of mental poison create painful emotional aches and pains.

This diet of deadly toxins will kill you, according to Saint Paul. He says to set "the mind on the flesh . . . is death."[4] If you continue to tell yourself distorted statements, you're going to have negative feelings and you're going to engage in negative behavior.

Persistent painful feelings are contrary to God's will.

God does not want His children to suffer depression, worry and intractable anger.

Did you know God wants us to be able to control our feelings and actions?

3. James 3:15.
4. Romans 8:6.

17

We can do it when we get rid of our misbeliefs and start paying attention to our self-talk.

A client named Bob sits in the therapist's office for his sixth therapy session. He fidgets with his hands as he talks. "It's getting so I feel tense and knotted up most of the time," he tells the therapist. "I've prayed about it, and I know the Bible says we aren't supposed to be nervous about things, but I can't seem to help myself. It's getting worse."

"You feel tense *all* the time?" asks the therapist.

Bob frowns. "All the time. Sometimes it's worse than at other times. I go to church but that doesn't help. Last Sunday morning in church I could hardly stand it. I wanted to run out."

"Why didn't you get up and leave?"

Bob is surprised at the question. "I couldn't do that! Everybody would stare."

"And suppose they did stare? Can stares hurt you?"

"They'd think I was crazy or backslidden. Oh, I could never just walk out of church."

"But you said you could hardly stand it. Do you mean that because you were with people, you felt you *had* to stay there?"

"Well, of course. I mean, they'd think something was wrong with me if I just got up and walked out."

"Would that be so bad?"

"Well, what if they knew what was going on inside me? What if they found out how tense and upset I am most of the time? I'm always afraid people will find out how uptight I am."

"What if they did know some of your inner feelings?"

"They'd think I was a kook, maybe. Or maybe I'm not a good Christian. After all, Christians are supposed to be happy and calm."

"Let me ask you something, Bob. If you had a friend who was having tense and nervous feelings, would you call him a kook or a terrible Christian?"

Bob shifts his weight, glances at the floor. "Of course not."

"You seem to think that what others think of you is more important than your own feelings."

Bob is quiet for a moment and then says, "I do want everyone to think well of me. I want to be liked, do what people admire—"

"Let's examine what you've told me so far and see where the misbeliefs are."

Bob shakes his head up and down. "I can see one for sure."

"What is it?"

"The misbelief that everybody should like and appreciate me. If they don't, it would be just awful."

Bob made a huge discovery that day. He discovered how important the words are that he tells himself. These words, or our *self-talk,* are what we listen to in order to hear our misbeliefs.

One of Bob's misbeliefs was that in order for him to be happy, he had to know he was acceptable to people and liked by them.

Misbelief: "I must please people. My actions must not cause others to disapprove of me in any way. If someone disapproved of me, it would be intolerable."

This string of related misbeliefs causes anxiety and an endless source of pain.

Truth: The Christian doesn't have to strive for the approval of everyone around him.

Bob needed to understand that the people he was worried about pleasing actually had no power to hurt him, even if they weren't pleased with him. He learned that very rarely do people get as upset with us as we imagine them to be. He was able to make dramatic changes in his thinking when he at last realized that the actual consequences of disapproval could never cause as much despair and anguish as his misbelief caused him. He also realized that it was God's approval that was most important.

Bob was one of the fortunate ones. He didn't land in a hospital or become dependent upon various drugs. He was able to take control himself.

You are the controller of your happiness and your unhappiness.

You'll be on the road to freedom when you take the first step and identify your misbeliefs for what they are. Learn how to recognize them and put them in their place as lies of the devil.

"You will know the truth, and the truth will set you free"[5] is a promise of Jesus. Let the truth expose your misbeliefs for what they are!

You can be free from such ugly feelings as bitterness, oppression, depression, anxiety, resentment, anger, over-suspiciousness and hypersensitivity. You can learn self-control and have fun while you're doing it.

In emotional and mental health, what you believe is *all important*. It makes a difference what you believe. Other people, circumstances, events and material things are *not* what make you happy. What you *believe* about these things is what makes you happy or unhappy.

If you believe it would be horrible if nobody talks to you at a dinner party, your mental and emotional self will react accordingly. Getting ready for the party you feel tense; on the way to the party you're feeling anxious. Once there you're sweating and uncomfortable. Your every impulse is to find someone to talk to, to be a part of things, to be liked. You wonder *why* you're so nervous. You may excuse your feelings by telling yourself, "Oh, those parties aren't for me. I'm basically a shy person."

Do you see how misbeliefs cause us to deny ourselves pleasure as well as the good blessings of life in Christ?

The misbeliefs in the above are:

1. It will be horrible if nobody talks to me at social gatherings (or if I don't know the people).
2. It's terrible to feel self-conscious and nervous.

5. John 8:32.

The truth is:

1. I can enjoy myself wherever I go, and I do not need to have someone to talk to in order to have a good time.
2. Feelings of self-consciousness won't kill me.

It's all right to experience these feelings.

Discomfort never killed anyone, but our misbeliefs tell us that discomfort is terrible, awful, wretched, horrible, when in fact, although not a lot of fun, it can be endurable.

What you think and believe determines how you feel and what you do. It is our endeavor to change the fundamental negative misbeliefs in you to the point where you will energetically and actively set about to get rid of them—permanently.

If you are a counselor, you can help people by helping them discover their misbeliefs. You can watch lives change and blossom before your eyes as people shunt their misbeliefs and actively inject the *truth* into their lives.

The question now is, do we really want to be happy?

2

Do We Really Want To Be Happy?

A very nice thing about changing your misbeliefs in order to be a happier person is that it will work for you *now*. You don't have to wait for months and years for a grand breakthrough. You can begin to change negative and unwanted persistent feelings immediately.

You have an advantage in working with a book like this. A misbelief that is frequently encountered in psychotherapy is that it is the *therapist's* job to make the client a well-adjusted and happy person.

Sometimes we expect a psychotherapist to treat us the same way a medical doctor does. You go to his office, present your body and your symptoms and he diagnoses your condition and prescribes proper treatment. Maybe you require medication or surgery. He puts you in the hospital. He operates. You take your medication, rest properly and soon you're much better.

Learning to be a happy, adjusted, productive and attractive person cannot be done for you in this way. Your therapist can't do it for you. He or she can't push a button and presto, you're no longer depressed or anxious.

It takes work on your part to be happy.

With misbelief therapy the client is informed immediately that the plan of action involves his hard work at changing the lies and misbeliefs which have victimized him.

Reading this book won't make you a different person, but *doing* something about what you read here will. We hope you have decided that you *can* change your emotions, you *can* be an adjusted and happy human being, no matter what you have experienced in your life and no matter what your circumstances are.

But I Can't Change the Way I Believe!

Some patients have no trouble accepting the truth that what they tell themselves makes them feel and act the way they do. But they may argue, "That's fine for you, a therapist, to say, but I can't change the way I am!"

The misbelief is, *others* can be happy, *others* can have an experience with God, *others* can correct and change their misbeliefs, *others* can be free from anxiety, depression and anger, but I can't!

Perhaps they have learned to believe these lies through critical and fault-finding parents, or maybe they have formed habits of comparing themselves to others and believing they come out on the short end. There may be many causes for such misbeliefs.

The chemical dependent believes he can't quit using drugs. The obese patient believes he cannot lose weight. The depressive neurotic says, "I can't help myself."

"I can't even if other people can" are crippling words. Changing your misbeliefs will change your feelings and actions. You *can* do it.

There may be some things in life you actually cannot do. Perhaps you cannot run a four-minute mile, hit a home run over the ball park fence, or kick a football sixty yards. But you *can* change your misbeliefs.

You may say to yourself, "Misbelief Therapy may work for others, but it won't work for me. I've tried everything and I can't make anything work in my life." Are you saying something like that? Let's change that misbelief right now.

As long as you're convinced that you can't change, you won't try. There have been many people who have believed they could never change. And yet, these same people have dug in and changed their misbeliefs in spite of themselves, and the result has been transformed lives.

Misbelief Therapy *will* work for you. It will work for you even if nothing else has because its effectiveness depends upon very explicit psychological laws which are as universal as the law of gravity. The law of gravity is evident when you drop something, causing it to fall straight toward the center of the earth. So it is with the laws governing the relationship between belief and behavior. What you believe affects how you behave.

Our Early Years

We talked earlier about the misbelief that all our problems stem from our childhood. This belief is widespread largely because of the influence of Freudian psychoanalytic theory, a magnificent but frequently erroneous personality theory which, a few decades ago, was generally accepted as the definitive word about human behavior. Now, however, psychoanalysis is not nearly as universally accepted among psychologists, and is losing ground among psychiatrists. Many excellent scientific investigations have demonstrated that it is entirely unnecessary to uncover the childhood antecedents of current behaviors in order to change them. Freudian psychoanalysis may actually provide an exercise to avoid working on changing behavior.

This is not to say that a problem is not better understood by looking into its history. Most therapists engage in exploration of the patient's past because it's important to a certain degree. We began thinking the way we now think at some time or another in our lives and often our thoughts and beliefs originate in childhood. Some of the primitive beliefs and behaviors that cause our unpleasant feelings and maladaptive behavior as adults were acquired in our early years. They may have been conveyed to us through the behavior and words of a significant person in our childhood. The impressions we learned in early years are important to us in order that we may change the misbeliefs we incurred then as well as the current misbeliefs we may have about our childhood.

Examining your early years may be important for the following reasons:

1. To discover your misbeliefs learned in childhood.
2. To discover your misbeliefs about events in your childhood.
3. To examine your self-talk:

    What did you tell yourself *then?*

    What do you tell yourself *now?*

When you were a child you may have thought it was terrible if you lost something or if someone was cruel to you, mistreated you or treated you unjustly. Examining your early self-talk may reveal some of your current misbeliefs.

Once these are discovered, you can go to work changing your present thoughts and attitudes. By working on the lies you tell yourself *now,* you can successfully learn how to be a happy person in spite of anything that has happened to you in your life.

What Causes Us to Feel the Way We Feel?

The state of your biochemistry can affect the way you feel. There are ways to change your biochemistry; one of the ways is through drugs. Another way to change is to begin maintaining an adequate nutritional base and a properly-functioning body. Your thoughts, too, can change your biochemistry. That's right; what you are thinking right now can actually change the chemical composition of your brain cells and the rest of your central nervous system.

Would you believe that the sentences in your self-talk can actually alter your glandular, muscular and neural behavior? It's true. That's what we mean when we talk about emotions.

Some psychologists are uncovering the fact that the way you *think* influences the way you *feel*. They speak of it as a brand new discovery, a modern-day revelation. Actually, this truth has been around for thousands of years. The book of Proverbs says, "*As he thinketh in his own heart, so is he,*" and "*The thoughts of the righteous are right . . .*"[1] and the book of Psalms gives us many words regarding man's thoughts and the material he puts into his mind: "I thought on my ways, and turned my feet unto thy testimonies."[2]

Our thoughts determine our behavior. When we speak of behavior, we mean not only our actions but also our emotions. Jesus kept telling people to believe, believe. Have faith, trust, believe. "According to your faith be it unto you,"[3] He said.

"Faith" is a noun that refers to the act of *believing*. Jesus' statement clearly teaches that we can expect certain things in our lives to take place as a direct result of how we believe.

What if you believe your life is hopeless and that you're nothing but a failure? "According to your faith, so be it done to you" is what Jesus said.

What if you believe that in spite of the ups and downs of life, you are not a failure, you'll never be a failure; it's impossible for you to be a failure! What if you believe that life is challenging and good and with Christ as the strength of your life, you're a winner through thick and thin?

1. Proverbs 23:7, Proverbs 12:5.
2. Psalm 119:59.
3. Matthew 9:29.

"According to your faith be it unto you."

Don't let anybody tell you that what you think or tell yourself isn't important. It was the main core of Jesus' teachings.

During the 1970s many experiments in psychology were done to demonstrate that changing misbeliefs resulted in changing feelings like fear and depression. Psychologists have spoken of "cognitive restructuring" or rational emotive psychotherapy or alteration of personal constructs. No matter which term the psychologists prefer, they are all excited about one major discovery, a fact which has long been known to wise men, including the authors of the Scriptures: *Change a man's beliefs and you will change his feelings and behavior.*

In order to accomplish our goals in this book and in life, we must systematically discover, analyze, argue against and replace with truth the misbeliefs in our lives.

Before starting, however, you will have to answer the question, do *you* really want to be happy?

If the answer is yes, then move on to the next chapter of this book, and the next chapter of your life!

3

Misbelief in Self-Talk

Yes! We want to be happy. The business of making yourself a happier and more fulfilled person can be a lot of fun if you let it be. Sometimes it may be a bit painful, as you become more and more aware of yourself and what you have accepted as you; but foremost, it promises to be an exciting time of discovery and renewal for you. Listen carefully, follow the scriptural course outlined, and trust the Lord to bring you through with flying colors.

Please get a notebook and pen now as we are learning new life skills and getting rid of the old destructive ways. You will be able to watch your own progress and learn much from the entries you make in your notebook. This chapter begins with an investigation of self-talk.

The Words We Say to Ourselves

Self-talk means the words we tell ourselves in our thoughts. It means the words we tell ourselves about people, self, experiences, life in general, God, the future, the past, the present; it is specifically, *all of the words you say to yourself all of the time.*

What are the lies and half-truths you repeat to yourself? Which misbeliefs keep you unhappy and upset? First you must learn how to identify the misbeliefs in your life.

Where do the lies and misbeliefs start?

The answer to that is in your *self-talk*.

Angie is a 31-year-old housewife who has been repeating negative things about herself most of her life. As an adult her negative self-talk has increased. "They're harmless words," she says: words like "Oh, dumb me. There I go again, being my old stupid self. That's just like me. What a dumb thing to do." "Boy, if I didn't have my head screwed on, I'd lose it for sure." "I can't do anything right," and "I have no interests." Finally, she says, "I'm really a nothing person. I don't see how anyone can stand me."

After many years' experience with such self-talk, she finds herself with a marriage of eight years hanging in shreds, her children disturbed and maladjusted, her friends few and her family helpless to assist. No amount of love and attention from anyone can convince Angie that she is a worthwhile and lovable person, although she says her biggest pursuit in life is happiness.

The words we tell ourselves are more important than we realize. If you tell yourself something enough times and in the right circumstances, you will believe those words whether true or not. Angie's jokes about herself were not really jokes at all. "Dumb me" said often enough is not funny.

"I can't do anything right" said enough times will find you *not* doing anything right, at least in your own eyes. Then, with a few negative remarks from those around you, such as, "You did wrong *again*," your belief in self-failure is reinforced.

If you tell yourself, like Angie, "I have no interests," you will find yourself behaving as if you had no interests. (That's impossible, by the way. Everyone is interested in something, no matter how trivial or unimportant it may seem.)

Psychiatrist Willard Gaylin said, "A denigrated self-image is a tar baby. The more we play with it, embrace it, the more bound we are to it." With each self-destructive sentence uttered, we ply another wad of tar on a developing tar baby which could eventually hold us desperately bound.

Listen to the words you tell yourself. Are you building a tar baby?

Angie believed she was basically an inept person with no skills or assets of any kind. She didn't see herself as personally attractive or interesting and believed she was not worthy of being loved or wanted by anyone.

Angie, by the way, is a Christian.

Rarely, if ever, did she tell herself that she was loved and cherished by the Lord of love. Rarely, if ever, did she count personal blessings. Rarely, if ever, did she thank God for her own special gifts and talents because she had been telling herself she had none for so many years she believed it. She had never told herself the truth, that she was unique and beautiful in the eyes of the Lord.

What Sentences Are You Telling Yourself?

In the following, check the words you tell yourself in the appropriate column. Be honest.

___ I am dumb.	OR:	___ Thank you, Lord, for giving me intelligence.
___ I am unattractive.		___ Thank you, Lord, for making me attractive.
___ People don't like me.		___ Thank you, Lord, for making me likable.
___ I have no talent.		___ Thank you, Lord, for the talents you've given me.
___ I'm miserable.		___ I'm content.
___ I'm lonely.		___ Thank you, Lord, for my friends.
___ I'm poor.		___ Thank you, Lord, for prospering me.
___ I'm nervous.		___ Thank you, Lord, for peace.

___ I'm uninteresting.	___ Thank you, Lord, for making me unique.
___ I'm no good.	___ Thank you, Lord, for your righteousness in me.
___ I'm sick.	___ Thank you, Lord, for perfect health and healing.

If you checked more sentences on the left than on the right, you need to change the sentences you are saying to yourself. Ask what you are measuring yourself against. Are you comparing yourself and your life with someone else who seems better in some way, or are you looking at yourself in the light of God's Word? D. L. Moody once said that the best way to show that a stick is crooked is not to argue about it or to spend time denouncing it, but to lay a straight stick alongside it.

The straight stick in the lives of Christians is the lovely and indestructible love of *Christ!* When our eyes lose sight of this dazzling truth, there remains only shadows to stare at. Shadows such as envy, jealousy, or comparing ourselves with others. Unhappiness or a state of discontent often is the result of longing to be different or to be in different circumstances, especially someone *else's.*

Not long ago, a poll was taken of 5,000 middle-class single and married men and women of average and above-average intelligence. The poll revealed that the single people were no more or less happy than the married people and the married people no more or less happy than the single. Common, however, was the finding that single people envied married people. Married people, on the other hand, reported envying single people. Many married people revealed they were happy because they were "supposed to be happy," not because they actually had feelings of happiness in their lives.

A single woman said, "I envy my friend, Jane. She's really happy. She has a husband, kids and a home. She has everything."

A married woman said, "I envy Connie. She has it made. She's free to come and go when and where she wants. Her time is her own; her money is her own. She's out in the world doing things. She's single and she's the really happy one."

What do you recognize in the words these two people are saying? Envy isn't usually realistic—it doesn't have all the facts. The words "I'm miserable and someone else is the happy one" are basically untrue. Everyone has some unhappiness in his life somewhere and sometime. Everyone has difficulties to face and problems to solve. Both Connie and Jane may have good lives, but they also have trials to overcome.

Picture a little boy jumping with delight as he tightly clutches a nickel in his fist. His mother gave him the nickel and told him to go outside and play. The little boy feels light and happy. But then he meets a playmate who has a quarter. His nickel suddenly loses its luster. He's not feeling so light anymore. He goes home and asks his mother for a quarter, and his mother gives him one. Now the little boy jumps happily once again until he meets another playmate, and this time the playmate has fifty cents in his hand. The little boy is crestfallen. His quarter looks pitiful next to two quarters. So back home he goes to get fifty cents from his mother. When he does, he runs into a playmate with a dollar bill . . . and on it goes.

If we do not find worth in what we are and what we have now, we will tell ourselves we are less important than others or we have less than others. When we tell ourselves these things, we create unrest within ourselves, and in striving to be or have what we think others have, we are always seeking after an invisible unattainable state of happiness which is always out of our grasp. Somebody somewhere will always be or have more than we.

Carol is a soft-spoken grandmother who lives in a modest home which is usually in need of repair. Her sons are successful businessmen and own homes twice the value of hers. Their wives are smartly dressed and have every convenience at their disposal. Carol cannot afford expensive clothes. She drives a second-hand car and takes her laundry to the laundromat. She is happy, out-going and content with her life. "Grandma is my bestest person!" her small grandchildren exclaim. Carol is not only adored by her family, but by her friends, neighbors and acquaintances. There is a peaceful, loving and unselfish quality about her which draws people to her. Her son marvels at how his mother avoids complaining. Carol knows the value of the words of the Apostle Paul, "I have learned, in whatsoever state I am, therewith to be content,"[1] and she lives them. Envy has no place in her life.

A young man who lost a limb in Viet Nam is able to praise God for blessings in his life and to lead a vital and productive life in spite of his loss. He tells himself, "I can do it. I have much to offer."

A middle-aged woman who lost her husband and three small children in a private plane crash finds courage and strength in Christ to go on and live a full life helping others and being a blessing to those in need. She tells herself, "I shall always miss my family, but I do not want to prolong grief and sorrow beyond the limits of God's will. It is His will that I be happy and useful—and I am!"

> A soothing tongue is a tree of life, but perversion in it crushes the spirit.[2]

Choose to say truthful things about yourself to yourself. When you hear yourself saying something false about yourself, *stop.* You can do it. Just say aloud, *"No. I don't want to say that. It is not true."*

Lorraine, a single woman of twenty-six, told us about the following event in her life: "I had moved back home to my father's house after quitting college. I had been gone from home for a couple of years and I didn't know anybody in the neighborhood anymore. It was all very strange. My father was nagging me to get a job, but I wasn't sure what I wanted to do. In the back of

1. Philippians 4:11.
2. Proverbs 15:4 (NASB).

33

my mind I thought it would be great to get married and get away from it all, but I wasn't even dating anyone seriously. Anyhow, one night I was in my room and I wasn't doing much of anything when I heard this little thought-voice coming from the back of my head somewhere. It said in a real high whiney voice, 'I'm sooo lonely.' I sat down on my bed and in a few minutes I heard myself sighing in a high, whiney voice, 'I'm sooo lonely'—just like I had heard in my head. It really scared me. I jumped up and shouted, 'I am *not* lonely. That's ridiculous. I am *not* lonely. I didn't mean that!'"

Lorraine was wise enough to recognize false thinking. She probably could have found enough evidence to support the thought of being lonely, but she chose to gather evidence to prove she was *not* lonely instead. She told herself out loud, "I am *not* lonely," resisting the temptation to verbalize the lying thought. She didn't start forming the tar baby which could have given her a lot of unnecessary sadness later on.

We can all tell ourselves we are lonely, inept or incapable at some time or another in our lives. A glamorous Hollywood actress, the envy of many women, was found dead in her bed with a suicide note beside her, "I am without hope." A magnificent poetess of considerable literary success believed she was a failure in spite of the awards her work had won and the acclaim she had achieved. At the height of her career, in utter despair, she committed suicide.

These illustrations prove the need for something more in life, some meaning and fulfillment beyond the external layers. They show a need for a spiritual relationship with the God who created us and His Son, Jesus Christ, who redeemed us. Release from self-denigration and hopelessness is available through faith in Him. The Christian finds within his grasp the dynamic results in such practices as:

> . . . whatsoever things are true, whatsoever things are honest, what-
> soever things are just, whatsoever things are pure, whatsoever things

are lovely, whatsoever things are of good report; if there be any virtue, and if there be any praise, think on these things.[3]

as well as:

Casting down imaginations, and every high thing that exalteth itself against the knowledge of God, and bringing into captivity every thought to the obedience of Christ.[4]

It is not pleasing to the Lord when we speak evil of anyone, or for that matter, when we speak evil *period*. To speak of yourself in a belittling or destructive way is, in His sight, evil.

Keep thy tongue from evil, and thy lips from speaking guile[5] (against yourself as well as against anyone else!). Depart from evil (saying evil words and believing evil thoughts about yourself as well as about anyone else!), and do good; seek peace, and pursue it.[6]

Pursuing peace means to choose it. You will never have peace if you are putting yourself down. The peaceful person is the one who is at peace with himself. Dag Hammerskjöld said, "A man who is at war with himself will be at war with others." When you like yourself, you will be free to like and appreciate others. When you are hard on yourself, you will be hard on others.

Write in your notebook the things you tell yourself about yourself every day. Listen to your thoughts and your words. Remember, any thoughts that reflect hopelessness, desperation, hate, fear, bitterness, jealousy or envy are the words and thoughts generated by demonic falsehood. These are the words and thoughts you will be changing and eliminating from your life.

Now, are you ready to go to work? Let's begin by examining some familiar maladies and the misbeliefs associated with them. See how many you can recognize.

3. Philippians 4:8.
4. 2 Corinthians 10:5.
5. Psalm 34:13.
6. Psalm 34:14.

4

Misbelief in Depression

One of the most familiar causes of psychological suffering is depression. Patients seeing psychologists and psychiatrists all across the world have such diagnoses as "depressive neurosis," "psychotic depression," "involutional psychosis," "manic-depressive," "psychotic: depressed," or "depressed," as well as other diagnoses with depressive symptoms. Worse, however, are the millions of people who, for various reasons, do not have the advantage of psychological or pastoral help, struggling through long miserable days in depression and believing there is no end in sight.

The Bible speaks of depression as the "soul cast down," and in Psalm 42 we can sense the agony in the words, "My soul is cast down within me" and "Why art thou cast down, O my soul?" Then triumphantly in 2 Corinthians 7:6 are the wonderful words, "God comforts those who are cast down."

The ancient church fathers had another word for depression. They called it "sloth." It was considered one of the seven deadly sins, on the same list with greed, anger and lust. Sloth was described as sadness of heart and reluctance to engage in any activity requiring effort.

Today we don't define depression in quite the same way. What exactly is depression? It can be described from various perspectives. If you looked at your biochemistry when you're depressed, your metabolism, the behavior of your smooth muscles and glands, you would see that it is not only your verbal and motor behavior that has depressive symptoms.

Depression usually occurs with some provocation. Most depression-causing misbeliefs enter the stream of self-talk after some loss has occurred.

Many times a patient will be unable to explain why he is depressed. "I don't know why I feel this way," he may say. "I just don't feel I can do anything at all. I just don't want to do anything. I cry a lot. I don't sleep well, and I don't have any energy or interest in anything . . . I don't know why . . ." His voice may trail off inaudibly or he may sigh, slump in the chair or just stare at the floor.

In spite of the inability of the depressed person to explain how he got that way, it is extremely rare for depression to occur without some special provocation. The misbeliefs that cause depression can become activated by a single event. This event represents a loss of some kind. Someone special or dear leaves or dies. Or it could be financial reverses and a loss of money. It could be physical illness, aging, an accident, stroke or loss of physical strength. Separation and divorce are frequent occasions of loss in depression, and situations where rejection, fear, and low self-esteem are triggered.

Any of these events can be an opportunity for the devil to slip a few suggestions into a person's self-talk. A college student may tell himself, "Boy, you sure are dumb. You failed your math exam. What are you doing in college anyhow? Look at all the money you're wasting. You'll never make it!"

The above example shows the three misbeliefs known as the depressive triad. Here they are:

Activating events followed by negative self-talk founded on *misbelief:*

37

1.	*Person devalues self:*	"Boy, you sure are dumb."
2.	*Person devalues situation:*	"Lately life has been a drag; nothing is worth doing; I don't know why I get out of bed!"
3.	*Person devalues his prospects for future:*	"You'll never make it! And you'll never be anything! Life is hopeless!"

If you repeat these things to yourself enough times, you will find yourself behaving accordingly. When time rolls around for another math exam, the student may panic, sinking to new depths of depression and worthless feelings. He may even quit school before the quarter is up because of his *misbeliefs*—not because of anything real or true at all.

A 37-year-old woman named Jennifer makes an appointment with a Christian counselor because she is suffering severe depression. Two months earlier her fiance called off their wedding and broke up with her. She can hardly go on, she says. Nothing seems worth living for.

At the first interview she appears attractive, intelligent and charming, although she insists her life is over and it's futile to go on.

She tells how she's lost interest in her job, how she has lost her appetite and doesn't want to do much of anything except sleep. "Life is a pain," she says listlessly.

Her friends had tried to console her with words such as, "You ought to be thankful you found out your boyfriend's true colors before it was too late and you were married to him. Then you'd be in a fine mess!" Or, "If that's the kind of person he is, you're better off without him!" and "You're better off staying single than married to a guy who is fickle and unfaithful." All of these words made sense to Jennifer, but they didn't help her.

Her belief system was already so jam-packed with misbeliefs she couldn't respond favorably to her friends' homespun common-sense advice. For several years she had been afraid of becoming an old maid. She had believed maybe there was something wrong with her, harbored fears and worries that maybe she wasn't attractive and desirable to men; otherwise, why was she getting older by the minute and still a single person? This engagement was the most wonderful thing that had ever happened to her, she told herself. This was really her last opportunity for happiness and wedded bliss.

Her self-talk had included, "If I blow it this time, I'll end up an old maid. That would be terrible. Awful! That would be so dreadful, I could never stand it." She worked hard at pleasing her fiance and doing everything "right." She was determined to be the greatest thing that ever happened to him, to be his "Miss Perfection," his Dream Bride.

Because she worked so hard at being what she hoped he wanted her to be, it made her feel all the more miserable when he rejected her. She told herself, "Even my very best stinks. I couldn't go through this again. It's all over for me. Nobody will ever love me. Even when I do everything I can to make a man love me, he leaves me. I'm the worst. The lowest."

You can see the familiar triad here:

1.	*Devalues self:*	"Even my very best stinks. Even when I do everything I can to make a man love me, he leaves me. I'm the worst. The lowest."
2.	*Devalues situation:*	"It's all over for me." (Meaning that since she is such a dud and since no one can love her, life is utterly unrewarding and negative—a pain.)
3.	*Devalues prospects for future:*	"I'll never be happy. I have no hope. It's all over for me. Nobody will ever love me."

Jennifer's misbeliefs are: she is a failure or worthless; she is guilty and inadequate; her situation is intolerable and lacking in everything containing hope; her future is hopeless and she might as well roll over and drop dead.

She has convinced herself through years of self-talk that to be unmarried is awful and to be rejected is the worst thing on earth, especially if it is by someone she worked so hard to please. ("How could he do that to me? And after I tried so hard? My best isn't good enough for anybody!")

39

Jennifer's awful fears and dreads have now come true. She tells herself she is the rejected castaway, useless, unlovable, ugly and hopeless. "To be me is the most awful thing I can think of."

Actually the only awful thing in Jennifer's life is the crock of lies in her belief system, her *misbeliefs*. They are awful, not Jennifer.

Her attributes are many, including an ability to teach handicapped children. She has many friends and is highly respected at the school where she has taught seventh grade for several years. But Jennifer is a Christian and Christians don't have to base their worth on achievements or attributes. Even without any achievements and without any special merit or attractiveness, the Christian can know for certain he/she is important and loved. Our lives have been bought and paid for with the blood of Jesus Christ and that means we're free from the pressure to *be* something, *do* something, *own* something, *achieve* something or *prove* something in order to be important and loved. We can do all these things or not do them and still be loved and important.

Jesus loved Jennifer so much that He was willing to die on the cross so she could have eternal life with Him one day, as well as a fulfilled life here and now. If Jennifer is as worthless as she says she is, then none of the things God says of His love for people can be true.

But His words *are* true and Jennifer needs to come to grips with them. According to God, Jennifer has worth and value and so does every other human being. The worth of a person is not based on success or accomplishment. It is not based on performance, achievement or even on how many people love and respect us. Our worth is based totally and solely on the declaration of God: "For God so loved the world." *God loves people.* No circumstance, no matter how bad it looks, can change this fact. The treachery and suffering of man is not from the hand of God, but from his own hand.

It is a misbelief to tell yourself that you are a failure. It is rare indeed that a person cannot do anything at all. Jennifer told herself that she was a failure because she had failed to hold on to her fiance. But that does not mean she is a failure in everything in life. She over-generalized.

The depressed person says that his/her situation is hopeless. "He left me and so I am nothing," Jennifer says. "My life has no meaning or value." Once the enemy, the devil, has a person deeply convinced of the lie that something or someone other than Jesus Christ is the foundation of life, he is open prey for the crippling pain of misbelief.

Our lives hold meaning because God loves us and because we are His. Our lives do not depend upon someone else loving us, staying with us, respecting us, noticing us or pledging their eternal devotion to us. It's nice to have friends and loved ones, but having them is not what makes us important. If you believe you cannot live without a certain person or that your entire existence depends on somebody else, you are setting yourself up to be hurt by that *misbelief.* If that person leaves you or because of circumstances you find yourself without them, you will tell yourself things like, "My life has no value or meaning." "Since I lost X, my world has no significance. I'm nothing now that X is gone."

That's not true at all. You are not reacting to X's leaving; you are reacting to your *misbelief.* We hear the popular songs with lyrics to the effect, You're-my-very-existence, without-you-I-wouldn't-know-how-to-take-air-in-and-out, I'd-be-an-empty-shell-and-a-worm-if-it-weren't-for-you. The romances on our screens and printed page teach us that love means to tell ourselves that all happiness and breath depend on someone else, on their reciprocal affection and acceptance.

Self-Centered Retaliation

One way some people have of combating depression is to tell themselves: "I'm *me,* I'm *somebody.* Nobody's gonna get in the way with what *I* want and need. After all, I'm a *human being. I'm me.*

I'm running the great show of my life. Yessir, *I'm* the star of this number. I'm me—*Numero Uno*, kiddo. You live only once and I'm gonna get all I can because I only pass this way but once and if I don't look out for *myself*, who will? If you love me, fine."

This philosophy is costly because there is no way to love others as long as the star of the great show is you—only you and you to the tenth power.

Jesus Christ is the foundation of our lives, not ourselves alone and not another person or persons. When we become God's children the great *I* dies and there's a change, sweet as morning, that takes place and we trade banners: the old used *I* for a shiny impenetrable *His*. Self-talk that degrades others degrades ourselves. We cannot undermine other people's importance and overestimate our own importance without trouble.

Burned and Staying That Way!

Many times when a person has been hurt by another person resulting from misbeliefs such as, "People should be nice to me and love me," he or she will react in still another way. Instead of admitting to anger or hurt, he or she will tell himself, "I'll never be so dumb as to let somebody do this to me again!"

You may be saying things to yourself you are not even aware of until you start consciously listening to yourself. The person who has been rejected by another person may believe that rejection is the worst thing in the world. To be rejected certainly is unpleasant, but it's *not* the worst thing in the world.

Listen to your self-talk and then engage in some honest and daring truth-telling.

Truth-telling such as, "This feels bad. I don't like it. It isn't what I wanted and it certainly isn't something that gives me pleasure." Notice we aren't lying about the situation—not saying, "Oh, this doesn't hurt a bit. Who cares if he/she rejects me?"

We're speaking the truth, not making stupid remarks about not having the emotions we were born with. When you cut your finger you say, "Ouch," right? When your heart hurts, it's truthful to say, "I hurt."

But you don't end the self-talk at that. Here's where so many counselors lock up shop. They advise, "Admit the hurt," then wave good-bye. But what do you do next?

You *continue* the truth-telling about the hurt. Here is some more truth to replace the lies that create anguish and leave it raw:

- It's true I'm feeling bad. It's only *unpleasant,* however; it's not doomsville.
- It's not doomsville because I'm not letting it be. I will allow some good healthy pain, but I *won't* allow anguish, misery, woe and disaster.
- I'm in control here. God has created me as an emotional being and so I can expect to have emotions. But God has also given me the fruit of the Spirit: self-control. So I will control my feelings and they can't control me.
- I am angry. I can, however, handle anger in the biblical, healthy manner. I do not lie to myself about this emotion and I do not try to squelch it or hold it in. I am also not a person of temper tantrums. I choose self-control.

When we lose someone or something important to us, we will feel hurt, yes; but if the hurt deepens to despondency and depression and remains that way for weeks or months, the cause is not the loss but misbelief. Two misbeliefs undergird this kind of despair:

1. God is not the source of life. Man is.

When we are despondent over loss, we are telling ourselves that the person or thing we lost is crucial to our lives and happiness.

The untruth lies in the fact that nothing and nobody but God is crucial to anyone. This truth is revealed in the first commandment:

Thou shalt love the Lord thy God and thou shalt have no other gods before Him.

To ascribe the all-sufficiency of God to any person is idolatry, and the basis for idolatry is deception and misbelief. James, the apostle, wrote, "Do not be deceived . . . every good and perfect gift comes from the Father of lights" (James 1:16, 17); those truly good and perfect gifts do not come from someone or something other than God. God is the giver of all good and all love. *He* gives us our relationships and our blessings. Now the second misbelief:

2. Since I lost X, my world has nothing of any significance in it.

Experience bears out the deception here. Many of us have told ourselves we "cannot live without" some person, object, scheme or notion. Then this adored "whatever" is removed from our lives and wonder of wonders, we recover. Some people without the skills we are learning in this book prolong their sufferings. They go on muttering destructive, irreligious, "without X I'm nothing" self-talk.

But many who have suffered loss in their lives recover and find satisfying and exciting alternatives. "I used to consider my health indispensable," an ex-football star says. "When I lost what I considered absolutely essential to living, I thought there was nothing for me to do but die." The handsome ex-athlete was in a car accident and lost both legs. He went on, however, to discover he had many interests in other areas. He graduated from college with honors and became a skilled musician. He is now married and working as a biologist. Although he encounters many problems as a handicapped person, these problems don't render him hopeless or helpless.

A famous artist was thrown into a Nazi prison during World War II. When it was discovered he was an artist, his torturers had his right hand chopped off. It could have been the end of his world, but he taught himself to use and draw with his left hand. He went on to a prolific career as a productive and skilled artist.

A person can lose his/her health, reputation, vision, hearing, legs, hands, even family members, money, homes, physical attractiveness, life goals and plans—and yet recover and go on living a wonderfully rewarding and meaningful life.

When you suffer a loss of any kind in your life, you are going to feel the sting of that loss; but the key to recovery is not to repeat that someone or something is of such importance that you cannot go on after losing it. You *can* go on. You *are* important. Martin Luther's great hymn counters this misbelief with the truth which stands the test of experience.

> Take they our life,
> Goods, fame, child and wife—
> Let these all be gone.
> They yet have nothing won,
> *The Kingdom ours remaineth.*

Part of the self-talk of nearly all depressives includes the statement, "The future is hopeless." Having lost her fiance, Jennifer was telling herself that she would doubtless have to live and die without marriage and family, that there would never be anyone that could replace him, and that even if she should meet other good men, she was such a loser she'd never be able to hold their interest.

The depressed person believes he or she can never be happy without the thing they now do not possess. Jennifer tells herself that she will never know true happiness if she doesn't get married. Many single people suffer with this misbelief. "Only through marriage can I experience life fully." If that sentence follows with, "I'll never get married. Nobody will ever love me," there's trouble. "All I can expect from life is frustration and unfulfillment" will be the words in the person's self-talk.

Examine those words and you will expose the misbeliefs. To begin with, no one can predict the future with certainty, least of all a person whose prediction is determined by the pain and hurt

45

of depression. We cannot predict that all of the events in our lives are going to be happy and enriching, nor can we predict that all ahead is gloom and despair.

Life at any given moment offers a mixture of pleasant and unpleasant, desirables and undesirables, fulfillment and disappointment. Some experiences are more gratifying than expected, but then some are worse than expected. Anyone predicting that life will be horrendous forever is as wrong as if he were predicting a nickel thrown through the air one hundred times will turn up tails one hundred times.

In actual fact, while nearly all depressed people tell themselves they will always feel devastated and down, *virtually all recover.* It is helpful to predict recovery if you are suffering from depression or if you are counseling a depressed person. That is because recovery from depression is in fact the most likely outcome! Speak the truth and say, "Even though I feel I have no hope, my recovery is assured. Thank God, these feelings of depression won't last."

Pray this prayer with us:

Dear Lord, thank you for giving me emotions. I'm thankful I can feel pain as well as joy. Thank you for setting me free from being a victim of my own emotions.

Thank you for caring deeply about me even though I'm sometimes unaware of it.

I choose now, in the mighty name of Jesus, to speak the truth to myself instead of misbeliefs. I am yours and so are my emotions.

In Jesus' name, Amen.

5

Misbelief in Anger

Marilyn had resented her husband, Jack, for years. At least once a day she told herself words like, "I can't stand this any longer," and, "I'm wasting my life with him."

Her husband was a minister who issued admonitions from the pulpit to abide in brotherly love, live in humility and honor your neighbor higher than yourself. At home he complained, found fault, made cutting remarks and compared his wife with younger and more attractive women. She felt insignificant and inadequate, and quite angry.

Marilyn didn't say anything to anyone about her feelings, although there were many clues which demonstrated how angry and hurt she really was.

She sat in her pew listening to Jack's sermons week after week as her insides twisted and her muscles tightened. She developed headaches which sent her to bed, sobbing with pain. Jack considered the headaches just a ploy to get attention. He preached about love and forgiveness from the pulpit and gave hours of loving advice in the counseling room, but at home he was impatient, critical and often cruel. His church face and personality was quite different from his home face and personality.

Years passed and Marilyn and her husband continued to appear in public as a happy couple, when actually they were worse off than the couples who came to them for help.

Many Christians try to deal with anger as a single moral problem. "Anger is bad," a sweet little Christian lady will tell her Sunday school class. "Anger is a sin, children, and you mustn't get angry!"

"We need to banish anger from our lives!" shouts the moralist. "Get rid of the anger in your life and you'll be a happy person."

The problem of anger cannot be dealt with so simply. Like taxes, anger doesn't just go away, even if you decide it ought to. And like your nose or your hair color, your angry feelings are part of you and your human nature.

There is a difference between being angry and expressing anger toward someone else. There is a difference between being assertive and aggressive. There is a difference between being capable of honest expression and being punitive.

Marilyn believed she had every right to be bitterly angry with her husband, Jack. She believed she had the right to *remain* angry as long as he refused to change his habits. She was ruining her emotional and physical health.

Both Marilyn and Jack had certain expectations of each other. They believed they had every right to demand the fulfillment of their expectations.

Specifically, Marilyn told herself the following:

1. It was shocking and intolerable to be treated unfairly by her preacher-husband.
2. She was right in *demanding* her husband treat her and their children with love, tenderness, consideration and kindness.
3. Since Jack was her husband, he *owed* her love. He should behave the way the Bible prescribes for husbands; namely, he should love his wife as Christ loved the church.

4. Her husband was terrible to criticize her and compare her unfavorably to other women. This behavior was dreadful and outrageous and absolutely intolerable.

The headaches were the cause of her visit to the Center for Christian Psychological Services.

"Marilyn, it sounds as though you're telling yourself you have a right to demand Jack be a good husband," Dr. Backus told her after hearing some of her symptoms.

Marilyn looked surprised. "Of course, Doctor. Don't you think I do?"

"Marilyn, when you were married you expected to have a husband who would be kind, considerate and thoughtful, but that isn't the same as having a guarantee from God that your husband would act that way."

"But why not? I'm considerate to *him*. I consider *his* feelings. I never compare him to other men. I build up his ego. I'm kind to him. Why can't he treat me the same way?"

"I don't know why Jack behaves as he does. I do know that you apparently haven't succeeded in changing him."

"But I can't take any more!"

Marilyn was now near tears and pressing her fingers to her forehead, indicating she was getting another headache.

"Marilyn, people rarely do what they *ought to* just because we want them to. Seldom is there a wife or husband who suddenly becomes habitually kind and loving just because their mate would like them to be that way."

"But he ought to practice what he preaches! What about all his talk about charity beginning at home? What about all that stuff he tells his congregation about humility and love? Sometimes I want to laugh out loud when I listen to him preach."

Tears now streamed down her face. She knotted her hands in frustration.

Whereas we don't want to make excuses for her husband's behavior, Marilyn needed to differentiate between what *ought* to be and what actually *is*. It is easy to look around us and locate disparity between what *should* happen and what actually *does* happen. We live in a sinful world. The fact is, as the Bible teaches clearly, "there is not a just man upon earth that doeth good and sinneth not." We can't find an environment on earth that is sanitized and sin-free.

Yet many people go through life giving themselves headaches, ulcers and high blood pressure over the fact that other people are not perfect. They confuse what *ought to be* with what *is*. Every time another person treats them unfairly, they tell themselves they have a right to get furious and stay that way.

"Marilyn, what sense does it make to tell yourself what Jack *should* be like?" Marilyn listened unhappily. "Since years of upsetting yourself over his faults haven't changed anything and have only made you miserable, wouldn't it be wise to start telling yourself the truth?"

Her eyes narrowed. "Which is?"

"Which is that it doesn't matter what Jack *ought* to be like or how you feel he *ought* to treat you. The fact is, he *does* treat you and the children in a way you consider unfair and inexcusable. Rather than constantly telling yourself how dreadful and intolerable your life is, you can decide right now to stop upsetting yourself over his behavior."

"But he treats everybody else better than he treats me, including the organist, the choir director, the Sunday school teachers, and the wives of the elders. What do you mean, upsetting *myself?*"

It wasn't her husband's behavior that upset Marilyn; it was her own self-talk.

"Suppose you were to stop telling yourself how terrible it is that your husband doesn't treat you the way you want to be treated. Suppose you tell yourself that while he may not do the things you'd like him to do and while it's an unpleasant situation, it's senseless for you to upset yourself over what you haven't been able to change."

She was quiet. "People have lived quite well with some very undesirable situations in their lives. Almost no one has everything just the way he or she wishes it to be."

"Yes, I know of many marriages having a lot of big problems."

"Nearly half of American marriages end in divorce. A good share of the other half are troubled."

If you're telling yourself you must have a perfect marriage in order not to be miserable and upset, you are telling yourself a misbelief.

Marilyn was taught how to get rid of her anger and headaches by learning how to change her self-talk. She learned the difference between the truth and misbelief. Here's a page from her notebook:

MISBELIEF	TRUTH
1. *It's terrible to have a husband like Jack.*	1. *Jack is my God-given husband, and, although I would prefer him to act differently, I can live with him without making continued demands that only go unmet anyhow.*
2. It's impossible to be happy with Jack as he is.	2. It would be nice if he would change, but it is not essential for my personal happiness.
3. I can't stand it any longer.	3. I can live a satisfactory and happy life even if Jack doesn't treat me as I want him to. My life can be fulfilling and enjoyable even if he never changes.
4. I'm wasting my life.	4. I'm not wasting my life. I'm believing in God to work in Jack's heart and make him the person He wants him to be. I am also believing God is working in my own heart, making me the person He wants me to be.

Marilyn did face reality. She discovered her husband's behavior was *not* terrible, although it was undesirable. She learned to discern when her expectations of others weren't realistic. It is not the end of the world if others are not thoughtful, kind or considerate. It's merely unpleasant.

If her husband's behavior toward her was not a source of happiness, she could find other rewarding activities and involvements in life to bring her satisfaction. She did not depend on her husband to make her happy by his acting the way she wished he would act. She could face up to him as he actually was.

It wasn't easy at first. Marilyn had lived with guilt over her anger for a long time; but little by little, as she felt better about herself, not only the anger but guilt feelings as well were diminishing. She began looking for the better qualities in her husband and appreciating things in him she had hardly noticed before. As a result of Marilyn's new behavior, Jack began to enjoy Marilyn's company. He had felt her disapproval of him for years and reacted by defending himself with attacks of criticism. When Marilyn stopped behaving in punishing ways toward him, he spontaneously reduced his critical and inconsiderate actions.

Often, but not always, relationships change dramatically when one person drops the misbeliefs that generate and perpetuate bitterness and anger.

Always the person who works to change misbeliefs will benefit even if the other person does not change.

The constant repeating of misbeliefs is what sustains and perpetuates angry resentment. Constant repeating of the truth generates peace and health.

Common Misbeliefs Connected with Anger:

1. Anger is bad and if I'm a good Christian, I will never get angry.
2. Anger always means to yell and throw things or do whatever else it takes to "drain off" the emotion.
3. If I do get angry, it's always better for me to swallow the anger than to express it.

4. I have every right to be angry when another person does not live up to my expectations. I have no choice but to stay angry as long as things don't change.

5. It is outrageous and insufferable when others do things I don't like, or if they fail to treat me as well as I ought to be treated.

You may have one or more of these misbeliefs. They are lies and distortions. They have, in each instance, the peculiar power to cause considerable suffering. Now here is the *truth*.

The Truth About Anger:

1. *Anger is not always bad.*

On the contrary, anger can be normal and has adaptive significance in appropriate situations. Remember, Jesus experienced anger. The simple emotion of anger is not always harmful or unloving. It is what you *do* when you are angry that has moral significance. Paul wrote, "Be angry, and yet do not sin; do not let the sun go down on your anger."[1] The Amplified version of this verse reads, "When angry, do not sin," which surely indicates we may sometimes feel anger. Paul is telling us that anger in itself is not wicked; that *what we do when angry can be sinful*; and that we should not allow ourselves to remain angry by continuing our destructive, resentful self-talk. He is telling us to deal with the issue *promptly*.

2. *Sometimes it's better to express your anger.*

There will be times when the Lord will want you to express this emotion, just as Jesus did on several occasions. He was genuinely angry at the buying and selling going on by the opportunists in the temple, for example. He saw ungodly people making ungodly gains in a holy place and this misuse of God's house angered Him.

1. Ephesians 4:26 (NASB).

As we can see from Jesus' example, it may sometimes be loving to reveal to another person that what he has done against you has made you angry. Matthew 18:15–17 really instructs in how to deal promptly with situations causing anger: "If your brother sins against you, go and tell him"—not "scream at him" or "prosecute him," not "kick things and slam doors so he'll figure it out." "Tell him his fault." It is a simple procedure. You can say, "What you did hurts me and I'm angry about it. I'd like to get you to stop."

3. *Anger does not mean yelling and throwing things or other intemperate behavior.*

Research on aggression[2] has demonstrated that if such behavior is rewarded and encouraged, the aggression increases; it does not decrease. The "steamboiler theory" held by some psycho-therapists concerning the emotions asserts that emotions are like steam in a pressure tank and must be released vigorously or they will cause a terrible explosion.

This assertion is not substantiated by the experimental evidence. Our emotions are not a kind of gas or fluid which must be expelled in order to prevent our popping all over the place in a million pieces.

Anger is behavior. Anger is responses of your body and mind to a stimulus. When the stimulus is withdrawn, the anger responses will cease—that is, *if* you do not continue to tell yourself how unfair and unjust your treatment has been and how miserable you are because of it.

If it were essential for our mental health to express all anger by shouting, screaming or punching something, then the Word of God would be mistaken in urging us to develop self-control. This does not mean we swallow anger and pretend everything is fine when it isn't. Sometimes it is healthier, wiser and more loving to say words like, "I am feeling anger right now. I'd like to talk about it because I feel it concerns us both."

2. Bandura, Bandura & Walters.

4. *I do not have every right to be angry when another person does not live up to my expectations. I do have a choice whether or not I remain angry.*

So many Christians keep asking God to free them from anger and they go through motions of asking for and receiving forgiveness. It doesn't occur to them that between their prayers they are telling themselves terrible things. "Naturally I'm angry," a person will say, "as long as so-and-so continues to treat me so badly."

There is no necessary connection between the behavior of another person and your anger. It doesn't matter how unfairly, unjustly or thoughtlessly someone has behaved toward you, you are angry because of your own self-talk. One psychologist tells his patients that the truthful statement to make when you're angry is, "I make *myself* angry." Other people cannot force you to remain in a stew over their behavior. This is something *you* do yourself. To take it one step further, you make yourself angry by what you *tell* yourself.

You tell yourself in words, images, and attitudes the very things that cause you to feel anger. "Isn't it terrible how Jim always keeps me waiting?" "It's disgusting and rotten that I'm the one who gets stuck with the job of mowing the lawn and raking the leaves while she sits inside drinking coffee!" "It makes me sick the way their dog eats better than a lot of people in this world."

When you are counseling a person who is angry or when you are dealing with your own chronic anger, it is vital to ask, "Why do I insist that someone else is making me upset when I am the only one who can make myself angry and keep myself angry?" If I'm angry I'm telling myself that something the other person is doing or saying is terrible; it shouldn't be that way; things aren't as I think they should be; and the resulting assumption is that it's awful, terrible, horrible, disgraceful, shameful and/or just plain horrendous. You can use only irrational notions to support such assumptions which are, in themselves, already irrational.

The truth is, such things are not horrendous at all. It is unpleasant when things don't go as you'd like them to or when someone says unkind words to you, but it's not awful or terrible.

5. It is not dreadful or even especially unusual if others do things I don't like or fail to treat me as well as I treat them.

We waste a lot of time, energy, and thought when we brood over the offenses of others. All of us have sinned, according to the Word of God.[3] Those who keep telling themselves how others ought to treat them confuse what *ought* to be with what actually *is*.

It would be nice if everybody was loving, considerate, thoughtful, kind and fair. The Bible warns us to expect sinful behavior in people since all men and women have chosen their own way. To those who are born into His family, God says, "Be ye perfect as I am perfect," *not*, "Try to make all those around you be perfect." God's perfection includes His perfect forgiveness and forbearance. It was His great compassion and love that took Him to the cross so that while we were yet sinners, He died for us.[4] So part of the perfection He desires in us is the same quality of forgiveness and forbearance.

The better you get to know another person, the more deeply aware of his or her shortcoming you will likely become. If you dwell on the negative characteristics, you can continually find plenty to criticize and be unhappy about. Your parents, siblings, spouse, children, and friends all have something about them you don't like. More than likely there is something about everyone you know that you would like changed.

The people in your life will not always be kind, just, loving, and thoughtful to you. You yourself do not always behave perfectly and fairly in every instance. But your heavenly Father loves you in spite of yourself. You can change your self-talk and love and accept the

3. Romans 3:23.
4. Romans 5:8.

people around you. He accepts them and so can you. (God does not accept sin. It's sinners He loves.) He loves the sinners thoroughly and sent Jesus to die on the cross for them so they could know God and be saved from the penalties of their sins.

When Anger Is Normal

The simple *brief* emotion of anger is normal. The anger which explodes into rage or stews in bitterness is maladaptive and sinful. Scripture gives two views of anger. "*Be angry, and yet do not sin*" it reads in Ephesians 4:26. Then James writes, "Be slow to anger, for the anger of man does not achieve the righteousness of God."[5]

Anger in itself is not always sinful. We have already mentioned how Jesus on occasion became angry. "And after looking around at them *with anger*, grieved at their hardness of heart, He said to the man, 'Stretch out your hand.' And he stretched it out; and his hand was restored."[6] None of us can go through life without ever having had the emotion of anger.

When Anger Is a Problem

Anger becomes a problem when it is made worse or perpetuated by misbeliefs—misbeliefs such as, "I must never get angry." This misbelief leads to the self-deceptive words, "I'm *not* angry," when one is quite plainly saying and doing hostile, angry things and even hurting others. The internal conflict and destructive behavior then becomes hard to interpret, identify and control. More self-deception develops and neurotic behavior follows. "I'm *not* angry. I'm a forgiving, nice person," says the bitter person between clenched teeth. He or she smiles, laughs and says friendly words while furious inside, refusing to confront the truth.

5. James 1:19–20 (NASB).
6. Mark 3:5 (NASB).

Christians are often prime targets for such deception. Many Christians think they must be nice fellows—always-smiling, above-it-all, super-people who are perpetually happy no matter what. When they are hurt and react with genuine anger, they hide it and cover it up with various shrouds, such as religious-sounding words, smiles, grins, shrugs, silence.

Jack and Marilyn, the couple at the beginning of this chapter, are examples. Jack resented Marilyn's obvious disapproval of him. He felt she was judging his every word and action, which made him feel uncomfortable and angry. He did not discuss his feelings with his wife, but his behavior showed how angry, hurt, and bitter he was. He felt her disapproval so strongly that he took every chance to show her she had bad traits of her own. Misunderstanding was compounded and walls were built between them. Neither one of them could discuss their hurt or anger, but their hostile behavior toward each other was vicious and cruel.

Both Jack and Marilyn refused to admit to angry feelings because they thought anger meant to yell, throw things, or act in a violent way. They were able to deceive themselves by thinking their angry behavior and bitter, resentful words were not caused by anger. Jack admitted, "I never hit Marilyn, nor threw anything or yelled, so I thought I was a person with the fruit of self-control. What I did do, however, was probably worse than yelling or throwing things. I belittled her with my sharp tongue or else I wouldn't talk at all. I'd stew in silence and not say one word."

Besides acting violently, silence is one maladaptive way to say, "I'm angry." Expressing anger by yelling, breaking things, stamping feet, or punching something is as dangerous as not admitting you're angry at all. Whoever said, "Never bottle up anger, let it out!" was missing the mark. There is a proper way to express anger, but erupting in riot is not the way. The notion to "let it all hang out" will never work the "righteousness of God." Untempered anger earned its position as number five on the ancient "Seven Deadly Sins" list because it *is* deadly.

Another unhealthy response to angry feelings is the "Fight! Fight! Fight!" attitude, not unlike the football fan cheering the team at a game. "Let 'em have it! Push 'em back, push 'em back, harder! Harder!" is the idea. The misbelief behind this notion is that the harder you fight the person or thing causing you to feel angry, the quicker the hurt will go away. But it doesn't go away. It gets worse, and so does the anger. One day you may find yourself screaming at the wind, hating and mistrusting even the dearest people closest to you for no good cause.

There is a healthy way to express anger. It is not through violence, nor is it by holding it in while pretending it isn't there.

The Healthy Way to Express Anger

Perhaps you've known someone who is chronically angry, always seeming to be nursing a grudge and ready to ignite any minute. Most of these people have one common trait. They are markedly uncommunicative and withdrawn. They are reluctant and shy about expressing their desires truthfully and openly. They are fearful of simply telling someone else what hurts them or how they have been offended.

Jesus teaches us appropriate and effective ways to have healthy relationships with others. When He tells us how to deal with anger and its causes, He says, "Go to the other person." Speak up honestly and openly, without accusing or manipulating the person. Tell him, "I am feeling anger right now. The reason for my angry feelings is that I heard you say such-and-such or you did such-and-such. These things have hurt and offended me and I feel angry."

Effective behavior such as this prevents you from becoming bitter and resentful, both sins in the life of a Christian, and will very likely get the attention of the other person. It will preserve rather than destroy your relationships. Prayerful assertive behavior that uses no harsh or hurtful words or action will bring a dramatic change in your life.

Each time you find yourself in a situation where someone aggravates you or hurts you, pay attention to what's going on in your mind. What are you telling yourself? If the words you are telling yourself are misbelief-centered, correct yourself immediately with the truth.

DON'T LET MISBELIEFS HAVE ANY ROOM IN YOUR MIND WITHOUT IMMEDIATELY COMING AGAINST THEM WITH THE TRUTH.

Arnold is angry at Ben because Ben just bought a new car and came over to show it off to Arnold who cannot afford a new car. Arnold thinks Ben is rubbing in the fact that he can't afford a new car. He tells himself Ben is purposely trying to show him up and make him feel bad.

Arnold has a couple of misbeliefs going, as you can see. One is that it is intolerable that Ben can afford a new car while he can't. (The truth is it isn't intolerable. It may not be desirable, but it's obviously not intolerable.) Second, it's terrible for Ben to rub it in by showing off his new car when poor Arnold can't have one, too. (It is not terrible. It may be a minor irritation, but it is not terrible.) Third, Arnold says self-depreciating words to himself and feels that he is a loser. If he doesn't check his misbeliefs soon, he'll really be miserable. (The truth is there is nothing at all wrong with not being able to afford a new car. True value does not depend upon what you can or can't buy; it depends on what you as a person are before God.)

In dealing with his misbeliefs, Arnold has to face them and replace them with the truth. But there's one point he isn't sure of and that is whether Ben is purposely trying to get his goat by showing off his new car. He decides to talk to Ben about it, which demonstrates some constructive behavior.

"Ben," he says with a serious expression on his face, "I'd like to talk to you for a minute about something that is bothering me." (Please note when you are about to talk to someone about your angry feelings to use an appropriate expression—not a face twisted with rage and blazing red with fury, and not a face smiling pleasantly and benignly as though you merely ate too much.) Face the person, use a normal tone of voice and look them square in the eye.

"Sure, Arnold, what is it?" Arnold's friend responds.

Arnold takes a breath. "I value our friendship and it's important to me that I be honest with you."

"Oh?"

"I want you to know I'm feeling angry right now."

"Angry? Yeah? How come?"

"I feel angry when you boast about your new car. You know I'd like to buy one, too, but I can't afford to. I get the feeling that you are kind of rubbing it in. Is this what you want me to feel?"

Arnold has opened the channels for positive and honest communication with his friend. He has avoided carrying around senseless bitter resentment and adding deeper feelings of low self-worth.

Anger should be expressed honestly, not hidden hypocritically. There is a difference between revealing the fact of your anger to someone and forcing him to taste the sting of your rage.

We can learn to admit to ourselves when we are angry and, furthermore, we can be free to express to the person who has hurt us how we feel, if we desire. It takes self-control and honesty. Raw emotions blustering loudly or seething silently won't do a thing but cause more emotional distress, not to mention accompanying physical complications such as headaches, backaches, high blood pressure, stomach disorders, and heart disease; and, most grievous of all, our Savior is hurt by our sin.

The Scriptures teach us to deal with our anger and the cause of it and to prevent the emotion of anger from running away with us. This constructive behavior is described in Ephesians 4:26, "Be angry, and yet do not sin; do not let the sun go down on your anger." Anger that is harbored and nurtured offers great potential for our acting in ways that are sinful and unhealthy. That is why it is important to identify angry feelings immediately and to be free to talk about these feelings.

The one person you should talk to at all times when you are feeling angry is the Lord. Confess any sinful anger to Him. Ask Him to show you your misbeliefs and allow the Holy Spirit to guide you into the truth. A promise we can count on is found in John 16:13: "He will guide you into all truth."

At times there will be no need to talk about your angry feelings to the person you're angry with because you will have taken care of it by talking it over with the Lord alone. With your cooperation, He often can remove anger from you in the privacy of your prayer closet.

Tackle your misbeliefs; replace them with the truth. Allow God to penetrate into your emotions and thoughts with His Holy Spirit of truth and you will find your self-talk, your thoughts, and your emotions with the presence of heaven in them. You're thinking, talking, and behaving to the glory of God.

When Someone Else Is Angry at You

No matter how effectively you learn to deal with your anger and its causes, you have to live in a world where other people sometimes become angry, and there are times when someone will be angry with you.

Here are some of the ways to deal with the anger of others:

1. Don't be upset every time someone becomes angry with you. It isn't a disaster. You *can* cope with it effectively.

2. Don't shape your behavior just to prevent others' getting upset with you; they will anyway and when they do, it's their problem, not yours.

3. Be careful not to reward the angry outbursts of others. Ignore them when they yell at you, but be very attentive when they speak reasonably.

4. Don't be intimidated. Speak up and say, "Please talk to me reasonably."

5. Be kind and loving. Just because someone is angry at you doesn't mean you have to be angry back. Say words such as, "I am sorry you are feeling bad. Can I do anything to help you feel less upset?"

6. When there is truth in an accusation directed at you, admit it. Don't lie and defend yourself. You don't have to be right all of the time. Say words like, "It's true. I wasn't using my head at all when I came over here boasting about my new car. I can see where I was just showing off and I'm ashamed of myself. Please forgive me."

7. Give others the right to be angry with you sometimes and don't be shocked and offended when it happens. If you insist everyone see and respect you as the Perfect Human Being With No Faults, you will be deeply disappointed, not to mention the victim of a gross misbelief.

Sometimes the anger vented at you by someone will have nothing to do with you. You may be merely the target of someone's frustrations and unhappiness. Learn to identify such things, refusing to take personally every word spewed at you. Always remember, the angry person's problem is *theirs*; don't make it yours.

The victims of child abuse and wife beating are increasing in number every year. Don't allow yourself to become one of these statistics by allowing the situation to go unchanged. If you are the victim or the perpetrator, there *is* help for you. You can be free from the horrors of uncontrolled rage.

Anger and Prayer

You're learning to listen to your own self-talk, and it becomes necessary to listen to your prayers as well. If you hear yourself complaining, pleading, begging, and reiterating grievances, it is time to take a new direction. Instead of praying the problem, pray the answer.

The words you say can move mountains. You need faith only the size of a mustard seed to do it. Jesus said nothing shall be impossible to you! Instead of, "O Lord, I just can't take it anymore. I've had it with this job. Nobody is nice to me; they're all so mean and nasty—the boss takes advantage of me, the workers are so stuck up and unfriendly. O Lord, it's just terrible," try this instead:

"Lord, I know nothing is impossible to me, so since I have to be at this job, I'm going to be there in your name. You tell me in your Word in Matthew 17:20 that my faith, even if it's small, can move mountains. I believe that, Lord, and I believe you can change me as well as my boss and the people I work with until we work in harmony. I know that you can lift this job from the level of drudgery, making it more than tolerable. Holy Spirit, move in my place of work and leave no heart untouched by your presence."

After praying like that, you wouldn't want to return to complaining; after all, you just gave the whole situation to Him. When you pray the answers instead of the complaints, you, too, will move mountains. Some mountains take a while to move, maybe even years, but you can manage that. It's a misbelief that God absolutely must answer immediately or else it's terrible and dreadful. Misbeliefs like that are anger-related and might start a string of other blatant misbeliefs, finally getting to the point where you're impatient and angry enough to accuse God of not caring about you or not existing at all.

When you pray God's Word and the truth, which you have substituted for your misbeliefs, you will begin to sense great changes in your personality and life. In Christ nothing is impossible to *you*. You can bring about great changes by believing those words and praying answers instead of problems.

Summary: How to Handle Anger

1. Confess your sinful anger to God, and receive His forgiveness.
2. *Locate and identify your misbeliefs.* What are you telling yourself that is not true?

3. *Replace the misbeliefs with the truth.* Eliminate the lies you've
   been telling yourself and start repeating the truth to yourself.

4. *Behave according to the truth.* Your old behavior resulting
   from misbelief has to come to an end. The old destructive
   ways of expressing or repressing anger, for instance, are gone
   now. In their stead is a person reacting according to the Word
   and will of God. You're honest, direct and sensitive to other
   people as well as yourself.

5. *Pray answers instead of problems.* You must believe that in
   Christ nothing is impossible to you, including the elimination
   of bitterness and anger from your life.

6

Misbelief in Anxiety

Suzie is stacking dishes in the dishwasher for her mother when she accidentally drops a glass and breaks it. Her heart pounds. She knows this means punishment. When she broke things in the past, her mother usually did three things: yell, call Suzie names, and spank. Suzie shudders in fear, thinking of what is to come. Then Mother enters the kitchen. When she sees the broken glass, she seizes Suzie by the arm, raves about the glass being fine crystal, calls her clumsy, careless and useless, and then wallops her.

The next day Mother again tells Suzie to stack dishes in the dishwasher. Suzie isn't very eager to do it. She tries to come up with an excuse to get out of the task. She says she has to go to the toilet or she has a stomachache and has to go to bed. Suzie feels anxious because she has been *conditioned* to feel that way. If she stacks the dishes, there's the danger of breaking something; and if she breaks something, she will surely get yelled at, called names and spanked, and that would be painful. In time, if Suzie has enough of these painful experiences—that is, breaks enough glasses and receives enough insults and spankings—she will develop anxiety that spreads into her very feelings of self-worth.

Pair these events with Suzie's social contacts. She goes roller skating and has trouble staying upright on the skates. The other children ridicule and tease her. In school and at home her brother calls her names in front of other people. Her father often calls her lazy and her mother yells when she doesn't perform according to her expectations.

Suzie teaches herself how to be anxious. When her playmates ridicule her, she feels pain; therefore, she feels anxious when she sees them playing on the ice skating rink or playground, as well as when she *thinks* about them. Her family's demands, which she cannot always meet, present additional anxious feelings.

So Suzie does something typical of anxiety neurotics. She begins to avoid the things that make her feel anxious. She begins to avoid contacts with her playmates. She avoids her family, stays by herself. She teaches herself that when she withdraws from situations that make her feel anxious, the anxiety level drops. This is reinforcing to her.

Carol is a 22-year-old person. She has spent several years of her life piling up anxiety responses, just as Suzie is doing now. She is riddled with fears and can't force herself to go out and get a job. She says she wants to get a job but she just can't get one. She has her own apartment near her parents' home which she rarely leaves. "If you could get out and get a job, you'd pull yourself out of the dumps you're in," her mother tells her over the telephone.

"I can't get a job," she protests. "I've tried and I just can't." In desperation, her parents insist she see a psychologist.

"I hate job interviews," she tells her therapist. "They scare me."

"Why is that?"

"Well, they're awful, that's why. The job market is tight and there are so few openings."

By her eighth session she is able to identify her thoughts and beliefs. She identifies her feared objects as other people. Her inability to land a job is not due to the job market but due to the anxiety she suffers at the *thought* of going out and being with people. She fears what the people could do to her.

"Carol, you said you hated being in crowds."

"That's right. I really hate it."

"What could a crowd do to you?"

"Well, they might make fun of me or laugh at me."

"Would that be terrible?"

"Yes, it would be terrible. It would be horrible. I'd hate that."

"Would it really be the end of the world for you if someone laughed or made fun of you?"

"Well—I'd hate it, but—I guess it actually wouldn't be the end of the world."

Carol didn't realize it, but she had just made a big and important step of progress.

1. She listened to herself and heard what was really going on in her mind.
2. By listening she realized she had been telling herself that to be laughed at and made fun of would be terrible, horrible. (Misbelief.)
3. She then argued that misbelief with the truth by telling herself that although she wouldn't like the situation, it would *not* be the end of the world.

People who suffer from anxiety tell themselves, "If the thing I worry about actually happened, it would wipe me out. It would be awful, horrible." Dr. Albert Ellis, director of the Institute for Advanced Study in Rational Psychotherapy, calls this "awfulizing." Anxious people do a lot of it.

Little Suzie does it when she avoids her playmates. "It would be awful if they were mean to me." Carol does it by avoiding job interviews. "It would be awful if I didn't do well."

Carol will realize that the idea of being in a crowd makes her anxious not because of the number of people or discomfort brought

68

by the press of a lot of people, but because she fears they might make fun of her or laugh at her. She will overcome this lie as she de-"awfulizes" the thought in her mind and replaces it with the truth.

Some common lies are:

- He/she/they might not like me. That would be terrible.
- I might not meet people's expectations of me. That would be terrible.
- I might be rejected. That would be terrible.
- I might fail. That would be terrible.
- I might say or do something dumb. That would be terrible.
- Once I've gained happiness, I might lose it. That would be terrible.
- Once I've gained love, I might lose it. That would be terrible.
- I might not look as good as other people. That would be terrible.
- He/she/they might not approve of me. That would be terrible.
- He/she/they might discover what a nothing I really am. That would be terrible.
- Nobody will ever love me. That would be terrible.
- I might be a terrible lover. That would be terrible.
- I might get hurt. That would be terrible.
- I might be asked to do something I don't know how to do. That would be terrible.
- I might lose everything I've got. That would be terrible.
- I could die. That would be terrible.

There are many more. How many of them can you recognize?

What Other People Think of Me

The central theme running through the misbeliefs in anxiety is that *what other people think about me is of such crucial importance that I must anticipate it in advance of all my actions. I must do all I can in order to prevent others from thinking badly of me. If they think badly of me, it will be a mortal blow to me. It would be terrible.*

Nearly all anxious people believe and tell themselves that they are in danger of other people's reactions to them. These words, like all misbeliefs, are lies from the enemy. While we are certainly glad if others think well of us and love us, we can still live very well if we don't have the affection and approval of other people. The Scriptures teach us to consider others in verses such as "Love your neighbor as yourself" and "Beloved, let us love one another," but that does not mean we are to strive and aim for the approval of everybody and drop dead if we don't receive it.

It's great to be liked. It is, in fact, more desirable to be liked than disliked. There is nothing wrong with learning how to be liked and appreciated by others. There are skills of personal communication which are beneficial to learn. But it is silly and destructive to believe that you *must* succeed in making everyone endorse you and everything about you. There is no reason why you cannot learn techniques for pleasing, influencing, persuading and changing the behavior of other people. But this is different from dwelling on such misbeliefs as, "I *must* be important to someone." It's nice to be important to someone, but it's healthy to leave out the "must."

The philosophy that says you should be liked and appreciated by one and all is not only silly, it's non-biblical. If you are learning techniques to please, influence, persuade, and manipulate people, what are your motives? Are you saying to yourself, "I *must* be important to someone—I *must* be liked—I *must* be accepted—I *must* be . . ."?

Let's assume your "musts" aren't fulfilled after all. Suppose people still don't particularly like you after you work diligently to gain their approval? Suppose someone actually hates the sight of you—outwardly rejects you? Suppose someone you respect and desire the approval of tells you to go fly a kite or jump in the lake or some similar brush-off? What do you tell yourself then? Because placed as paramount in your gallery of "musts" is the notion that everybody should approve of and like you, you'll probably respond to rejection with such miseries as, "I'm really a loser," or, "What a failure I am," or, "I'm a real nothing," or, "I'll get them for this. I'll show the world!" "I don't need *anybody!*"

The Bible does not teach us to please everybody on earth. It does not tell us to work overtime trying to get people to love us. Jesus never told us to go out and take a course in how to get people to like us. He told us to love *Him,* trust *Him,* have faith in *Him,* glorify *Him,* and to genuinely care about others.

The price an anxious person pays to please people is too great. Jesus, above all others, demonstrated that if a person is really serious about pleasing God, there will be times when his behavior will be just the opposite of what others expect of him. Jesus himself wasn't loved by everyone and still isn't. Jesus wasn't accepted by everyone when He lived, and He still isn't. Many have found fault with Him. When He was alive on earth He made the leaders and molders of public opinion quite upset with His social behavior. He befriended prostitutes and thieves and sought the company of traitorous tax gatherers. This did not make Him Mr. Popular with the religious folk. In fact, many of the things He did didn't win Him friends. People found fault with the way He talked and worshipped; they didn't like what He said, didn't like His friends, didn't like what He did—they even criticized the way He *ate.* But He wasn't devastated by what others thought of Him because He kept His eye on the Father and doing His will.

In fact, He had joy through it all and says to us, "*My* joy I give to you." Jesus didn't live to please people. He lived to please His Father in heaven.

Nobody other than you has the power to make you miserable. That power is yours alone.

71

You make yourself miserable by the things you tell yourself. Sometimes, however, an anxious person cannot define what it is that is making him anxious. The term *anxiety* covers a large number of behaviors, including cognitive activity (such as worrying, fretting, obsessing) as well as physiological events appropriate under stress (dry mouth, perspiring, rapid heartbeat and respiration, dizziness, light-headedness, tremors, butterflies in the stomach, tense muscles). Anxiety is ordinarily defined as fear in the absence of actual danger. The event a person fears is highly unlikely to do to him what he fears.

Anxiety is:

1. Fear in the absence of real danger.
2. Overestimation of the probability of danger and exaggeration of its degree of terribleness.
3. Imagined negative results.

The acrophobic person has a fear of heights and is afraid he will fall from the highest floor of a tall building to his death even though he is indoors with the windows closed or standing on a heavily screened observation platform. He grossly overestimates the likelihood of falling. Granted, it certainly wouldn't be a pleasant event if a person were to trip off the edge of a high building and plunge twenty floors to the pavement below, but the likelihood of its actually happening is extremely remote. In spite of that, the acrophobic person is horrified that such a thing might happen to him. His life can be made miserable because of his fear of heights. Driving along a mountain road may be a living nightmare to him. He may get hysterical if he has to climb a ladder or scale a catwalk. Just the thought of a high plane can bring a cold sweat to his brow. He is trapped by this fear in spite of the fact that he is actually in no danger at all.

The zoophobic is another person with exaggerated fear. His anxiety, due to imagery, is related to animals and he is deathly

72

afraid of them. He may turn pale and tremble in the presence of a tiny kitten. What he is doing is *exaggerating* the degree of evil he would suffer if the kitten were to jump on him and bite or scratch. He may imagine being clawed to death, disemboweled, or being suffocated by it. In reality, he is in very little danger at all. The zoophobic realizes that most domestic pets are not dangerous, but he is tormented by images of danger.

The claustrophobic person is afraid of small places. Elevators, small rooms without windows, crowded narrow hallways and other enclosed areas will be an agonizing torture for this person. He is afraid that if the building were to catch fire or if some disaster were to occur, he couldn't get out fast enough. He over-stresses the likelihood of these improbable events happening. He is tormented by this fear.

Another person who experiences agonizing anxiety is the agoraphobic person who is fearful of open places. He is afraid that if he goes to these places, he will have an anxiety attack at being there and be unable to escape. He tells himself he will become so anxious in such places that his heart will race, his breath will come in gulps, his limbs will tremble, his head will swirl, he'll black out and lay squirming on the ground making a public spectacle of himself. Maybe he'll die or maybe he'll get carted away to some hospital where he'll be pronounced hopelessly insane.

How probable is such an event?

Little Suzie at the beginning of this chapter has become an agoraphobic. She sits in the big leather chair of the consulting room, her eyes darting back and forth at the furnishings and out the window.

"Suzie, is it true you haven't been to school for several days?"

"I guess so. I'm never going back."

"Never?"

"Never. I hate it. It's too big. My other school wasn't so big."

"Did you like your other school better?"

"No. I hated that school, too. I don't want to be around so many people. They make me nervous."

"What happens when you become nervous?"

"I don't know. I just get sick, I guess. I feel sick."

"Where do you feel sick?"

"Everywhere. I just feel sick. I feel like I'm going to faint or lose control. Like I'll lose control."

"What do you mean by that, Suzie?"

"I'll just lose control, you know, like start screaming or crying or maybe I'll fall down or something and lose control."

Little Suzie, whose parents can't understand how they could possibly have such a "disturbed child" wonder if she is brain damaged. There is nothing wrong with Suzie's brain, however. She is a bright child who suffers anxiety at phobic proportions. At first she doesn't want to receive psychological help, but after a few sessions she begins to respond and she likes her therapist.

"Suzie, what would happen if you actually did lose control, as you say, in the middle of a crowd?"

Her eyes widen and the pulse beat at her temples quickens. "Oh, I uh—I would lose control. I'd—I'd—I don't know, maybe go crazy."

"Do you *really* think you would go crazy?"

"Do you think I would?"

"No, I don't."

She is quiet for a moment. She is fumbling with her hands. "I uh—I don't know. I'd lose control in front of all those people. In front of the other kids. It would be the worst. The worst."

"Would it really? What would be so bad about that?" She wants to laugh, but she just groans. "Oh, that would be so terrible."

Several sessions later, she is able to honestly say to her therapist, "I suppose it wouldn't be the end of the world if I lost control."

"And do you *really* believe you will lose control?"

"Well, I don't know. After all, we did go to school twice last week and I didn't lose control. I went this morning—"

74

"Is it unpleasant to be around all those kids?"

"Yes, it's unpleasant."

"It's endurable, though, isn't it? I mean, a thing can be unpleasant and still endurable, can't it, Suzie?"

Suzie smiles her brightest smile since she has been coming for therapy. She shrugs then and says, "I s'pose. I just never thought that something could be unpleasant and that I could still get through it."

"Are you willing to go to school again tomorrow?"

"I think so."

The "terrible" consequences Suzie imagined were based on nothing but anxiety. Some people's lives are organized around the effort to avoid anxiety. The fear of fear consumes their waking hours and anxiety about anxiety brings such tension and stress that it becomes self-fulfilling. The agoraphobic cries like Job, "The thing which I greatly feared is come upon me."[1] The misbelief is exaggeration of the badness of the anxiety attack. For even though it may be truly uncomfortable, it is not likely to do a person any harm.

We don't want to make the answers to Suzie's problem sound simplistic, and we don't want you to get the idea that phobias are cured miraculously after a few little talks with a Christian psychotherapist. Suzie has come a long way, though, and is on her way to true recovery. She is beginning to understand and *act* on the truth. She is learning how to argue against her misbeliefs. Her parents' unrealistic expectations of her, rejection from her brother and friends, as well as failure at sports and schoolwork all contribute to her anxiety responses. The wonderful fact is, however, she will not have to wait until she is an adult to learn the skills that make for a healed and normal life. She is learning them now with God's help.

The love of God reaches into Suzie's fears. This love surrounds, engulfs and pierces into her soul where her emotions and thoughts live. She imagines the Lord accompanying her to school; she sees

1. Job 3:25.

Him standing beside her in the school gym softly whispering, "I'm with you always, Suzie"; she chooses to replace some of the self-condemning lies she has believed with such truths as: The same spirit that raised Christ from the dead dwells in me.[2] Gradually and slowly, Suzie will take part in the youth group at church and she will be a sparkling star for the Lord whom she is finding to be very real.

Perhaps Suzie has suffered more than most little girls in the sixth grade, but she has learned something many adults are still groping to discover. *Even though things may be unpleasant, I can live through it without falling apart* and *things are only as unpleasant as I tell myself they are.*

Let's look at the major misbeliefs in anxiety.

1. If the thing I worry about were to happen, it would be *terrible*.
2. Even though the likelihood of the *terrible* happening to me is utterly remote, I believe it's actually inevitable.

Most of our anxieties do not reach phobic proportions. You may feel tense and anxious when you have to get up and give a speech or when you are in a new and unfamiliar situation that demands your best; but more than likely, your reactions won't reach phobic proportions. You may think your legs are turning to putty and your stomach is popping with flying objects, but you do eventually recover.

An actor tells himself on opening night of his play that he will surely have a heart attack before the curtain goes up. He perspires, his hands are cold, his feet feel numb. He has difficulty breathing. "I'll never live through it," he tells the floor. "I don't remember a word of the script. I'm sick all over."

Two and a half hours later, when the curtain rings down, he feels great. Why? He got through it. He shows us one of the best cures

2. Romans 8:11.

for situational anxiety. Avoid it and you'll increase the anxiety. Face it and go through the anxiety and you'll remove it.

It may be unpleasant, but who ever told us all of life was supposed to be pleasant? The actor somehow pushed one foot in front of the other and got himself out on stage at his cue. From then on, he was okay. He got through it, and on top of it—got through it well. Whether or not the play was a critical success is not important. What is important here is that he plunged through his anxiety and didn't turn back.

When you are feeling anxiety, stop and ask yourself:

1. What am I telling myself is terrible?
   (The actor tells himself he'll forget his lines, he'll do a bad job in the play. He thinks that's terrible.)
2. Will the results really be as terrible as I tell myself they'll be? The actor says *terrible* things will happen if he forgets his lines or does a bad job.)

Now argue the case—like this:

1. It's not terrible. It may be unpleasant, but that's a long way from *terrible.*
   ("Some of the things that I believe to be absolutely terrible really are only annoying.")
2. Even if what I fear were to happen, it wouldn't be *terrible.* It might be unpleasant, but it surely wouldn't be the end of the world or me.
   ("If the worst happened, the consequences wouldn't really be as bad as I've been telling myself.")

Avoidance Behavior

The actor could have refused to go on stage the night his play opened. He could have chosen to run away from the unpleasant feelings he was experiencing. But he didn't. He forged ahead, plowed through his anxieties—and afterward? He felt good.

Many situations in your life may be less than pleasant. In fact, oftentimes you'll be faced with problems that seem to be insurmountable. Avoiding the problem or situation usually makes it more intense. Avoiding anxiety is not the way to get rid of it. Tell yourself:

1. Even though I'd like to avoid the circumstance or situation, I will *not*. Avoidance behavior will only increase my anxiety. I will go ahead, experience the unpleasant feelings, and I'll get through it.
2. I do not have to be afraid of unpleasant feelings. They are a part of life and they won't kill me. It's acceptable to have unpleasant feelings at times.

Margaret is a beautiful woman of forty with the energies of a teenager. She busies herself caring for the needs of her family as well as working a full-time job outside the home. She has several hobbies and is active in her church as a prayer group leader and Sunday school teacher. She is well loved by those closest to her and has many friends and acquaintances. She has one problem: she is deathly afraid to drive a car and refuses to learn how.

This problem was magnified when her husband decided it was time to move to a larger home in the suburbs. Margaret would no longer have the convenience of the city buses to help hide her fear of driving. She would no longer have the familiar busy routine with which she felt safe and secure. She was faced with the threat she dreaded most: sitting behind the driver's wheel and driving a car on dangerous streets and highways. The thought was horrible. It nearly cost her her marriage.

"I won't move," she told her husband flatly.

"But we'll move into a bigger and better home," he tried to reason. "We'll have everything you could want."

"I'm not going."

"But why not? What's wrong?"

"I hate the suburbs."

Her husband could not understand her attitude. He attempted a rational discussion. "But you've always said how much nicer it would be to live in the suburbs. The children would have more outdoor freedom, we'd have a more modern home with more space, it would be more quiet than the city . . ."

"I don't want to talk about it. If you want to move, go ahead. You move without me, though."

"I don't *want* to move without you. That's a foolish thing to say."

"If you really loved me, you wouldn't do this to me."

"Do *what* to you?"

Her husband was unaware of the proportions to which Margaret's anxieties had grown. She had been able to develop her fears without revealing how painful they were. Her lies were, "If I drive a car, I'll have an accident and that would be terrible. I could kill someone. Or I could be killed."

Margaret and her husband sought professional marriage counseling and the truth emerged. Margaret's fear of driving was deeper than they realized.

Very gradually and over a long period of time, Margaret was able to overcome this fear. Eventually she was able to take driving lessons and even own her own car. She was able to *get through* her unpleasant feelings; she *could* do the thing she dreaded.

But how does Margaret or anyone else experiencing intense anxiety get to the point where their fears pass? The answer is to *listen* to the words you tell yourself, *argue* against those words, and *replace* the misbelief with the truth.

In a very short time Margaret was able to see her misbeliefs clearly. They were: "Driving cars is the most dangerous thing a person can do. I might do something stupid or make a mistake, costing a life. That would be the most terrible thing I can think of."

She then taught herself to challenge such nonsense: "Driving cars is *not* the most dangerous thing a person can do. Living without Jesus is more dangerous. Furthermore, if I make a mistake, I will handle the consequences."

She learned to speak the truth to herself, "Even though it is anxiety-arousing for me to get behind the wheel of a car, I *can* do it." Gradually she progressed from sitting behind the wheel to starting the engine. ("I *can* do it. In Christ nothing is impossible!")

Then, with someone sitting beside her in the front seat, she would put the car into drive, step gently on the gas and drive only to the end of the driveway; then she would brake, put the car in park, and turn off the engine. ("I *did* it! I drove the car! I got through it! Thank you, Lord.")

The next day she repeated driving to the end of the driveway. She did this for three days. We asked her how she felt driving to the end of the driveway for the fourth time.

"I felt fine."

"No anxiety?"

"No, not really. I felt fine about it."

"Why do you think you felt fine about it?"

"Well, I knew I could do it. I had done it three times before and it didn't do me in. I guess I just felt confident it wasn't going to be that terrible."

We were delighted and congratulated her. Then we asked, "Are you ready to drive to the corner?"

Margaret made the drive to the corner. She did it several times with someone with her and then she soloed. "I did it!" she exclaimed. "I never dreamed it would be possible."

Most anxieties are related to four things:

1. Dread of making public mistakes.
2. Fear of making someone else angry or upset.
3. Losing love.
4. Physical pain and death.

These fears are exaggerated and often needless. In reality, *you* create anxiety, not situations or events. Anxiety is brought about by your telling yourself something is *terrible*.

What does "terrible" mean? Usually it means something far worse than you think you can endure. You tell yourself the "terrible" is beyond human endurance, worse than anything on earth. Truly, nothing of this sort exists.

"Terrible" is something that you firmly believe ought not to be. *It's terrible; therefore it must not exist.* This, too, is a misbelief.

Inconvenient, annoying, unfortunate, unpleasant stimuli will always exist. *You,* however, control your own feelings. *Thinking creates feelings.* You'll never get rid of every unpleasantry around you, but you can gain the skills to handle them effectively. The mistaken belief that life should be sweetsey, nicey, and without problems will make you quite miserable. With these ideas in your mind, you will seek to avoid or run from trouble rather than overcome it.

Jesus tells us quite clearly that we will encounter negatives in this world and that there will be problems, trials, and temptations of all sorts. He said, "In the world you shall have tribulation." He warned us of a devil, the enemy of God who seeks to destroy man; but then He said triumphantly, "But be of good cheer; I have overcome the world."[3] We can be free of crippling anxiety when we rest in this beautiful fact: In Christ, we are safe, loved, protected, watched over, and one day bound for eternal glory.

Getting rid of your anxiety means to (1) minimize the danger you tell yourself you're in (remember, your fears are exaggerated); (2) realize *you* create your anxiety (you create your own misbeliefs); (3) dispute these misbeliefs, challenge them ("is this really as terrible as I'm telling myself?"); (4) replace the misbeliefs with the *truth*. Don't worry about how weak you think you are. Jesus said, "My strength is made perfect in weakness."[4]

3. John 16:33.
4. 2 Corinthians 12:9.

Here are some words of truth with which to argue those lies:

For our light affliction, which is but for a moment, worketh for us a far more exceeding and eternal weight of glory (2 Cor. 4:17).

Behold, I give unto you power to tread on serpents and scorpions, and over all the power of the enemy: and nothing shall by any means hurt you (Luke 10:19).

And I say unto you, Ask, and it shall be given you: seek, and ye shall find; knock, and it shall be opened unto you (Luke 11:9).

Submit yourselves therefore to God. Resist the devil, and he will flee from you (James 4:7).

Greater is He that is in you than he that is in the world (1 John 4:4).

But they that wait upon the Lord shall renew their strength; they shall mount up with wings as eagles; they shall run, and not be weary; and they shall walk, and not faint (Isa. 40:31).

Let's pray together, "Create in me a clean heart, O God; and renew a right spirit within me." And now let's expect great things as He answers our prayer. Anxiety will no longer have controlling power over you.

7

Misbelief in Lack of Self-Control

Ann's eyes are downcast, her voice low and quivering. "It just all seems so hopeless . . . sort of, well, like I'll always be in this awful rut . . . like there's no way out . . . I just can't seem to get going on anything . . . I mean, God knows I pray and pray, but nothing ever seems to happen. My prayers are just never answered. It's just so . . . hopeless."

Tears slide down her pale cheeks. "I expected Jesus to change me when I gave my life to Him five years ago, and He certainly has—that is, so many things in my life are really changed for the better and He has blessed me in so many ways—but there's one thing I just can't seem to get anywhere with and that's self-control. You know what I mean?"

She continues miserably. "See, I need to get a job, but I just don't go out and look for one. I always make some excuse for not going out, although I do read the want ads and sometimes I find certain jobs that look good, but I need to lose weight, as you can see, at least 30 pounds; I want to get down to 125 pounds, but I just *can't do it*. I've prayed and prayed about this, and then I just can't seem to get going. . . ."

For the next 40 minutes Ann delivers a barrage of "can't do's," each one prefaced by the sentences, "It's all so hopeless" or "I can't," "I lack," and finally, the crunch: "God doesn't care about me. If He did, He'd change me."

David is a handsome 35-year-old used-car salesman. His twinkling eyes and bright smile fade as he explains, "It's like I'm a victim or something. You should see the paper work I've got to do—a ton of it—and I just can't get to it. My discipline stinks. And that's not all. I'm late everywhere I go. I oversleep, I do lots of things I really shouldn't do. I've always got a good excuse, but this last month being late cost me about $3,300. The month before my being late cost me plenty, too. I can't keep on like this!"

Shirley dabs her cigarette out in the already overflowing ashtray of butts. "I'd love to quit smoking, but I don't have the self-control. I'll probably croak of lung cancer and my dying words will be, 'Got a light?' I've tried quitting and once I lasted three months without taking a single drag on a cigarette, but here I am, smoking two packs a day. Some people have the self-control, and others, like me, don't."

For most of us there is no easy way out of life's difficulties and responsibilities. It's a lot easier to blame Jesus for our not going out and getting a job than it is to do something about the problem. It's a lot easier to oversleep and avoid the monumental task of long-overdue paper work than it would be to sit down and begin work on it. It's a lot easier to keep on smoking than it is to quit. It's a lot easier to sit in a comfortable chair with a bag of potato chips watching TV than it is to engage in a series of physical exercises or to diet.

Elaine, a distraught mother of two children, cries, "I feel like I'm a rubber ball, just bouncing along where I'm thrown. I make all sorts of new resolutions—like, how I'm going to get into reading the Bible more; or, how I'm going to start exercising to get rid of this flab on my body; or, how I'm going to get the house clean by noon and then do this or that. But then I'll sit on the phone all morning, or watch soap operas instead of reading my Bible, or I'll eat a dish of ice cream wishing I were thin. Where is self-control in my life? Aren't I supposed to have self-control? Isn't that one of the fruits of the Holy Spirit?"

Many people try drugs, hypnosis, and even surgery in their desperate flight from facing responsibility and difficult tasks, but seldom do these methods bring lasting results or the happiness so passionately sought.

We asked Ann to face the reasons why she couldn't go out and get herself a job. "Well, I don't know. I just can't."

"Are you afraid to apply for a job?"

"Yes, I suppose so. I'll probably be turned down."

"But you said you were qualified enough to get any number of jobs."

"Yes, that's true. But that doesn't mean anything. I guess I'm just afraid of rejection."

"But why are you afraid of rejection? What's so bad about being rejected?"

"Are you kidding? What's so *bad* about rejection? That's the worst thing in the world. A person likes to feel accepted and wanted."

"You said you're qualified enough to land a good job. You said you've had two years of business school and that your skills are good. What makes you think you'll be rejected when you apply for a job?"

"Well, they want pretty girls . . ."

"Now wait a minute. Are you telling yourself you're not *attractive* enough to get a good job?"

"Isn't that obvious? Look at me, I'm at least 30 pounds overweight."

Notice the self-talk here. Ann tells herself she can't get a job, but then reason tells her she probably could because she does possess the skills to get the kind of job she'd like. So then she tries another lie: she's not attractive enough. (If this were true, we'd have a world with no overweight or unattractive people working.)

"I used to have a body of a model. I was what they called a real knock-out. Now I'm really disgusted with myself."

"And is it important for you to be a knock-out in order to feel good about yourself? Suppose what you consider attractive isn't attractive at all? Suppose it was considered gauche for a woman your height and build to weigh less than 200 pounds?"

"I weigh 140 now."

"Well? What would you do?"

"I'd probably gain weight."

"And if you did gain the weight, putting yourself 75 pounds heavier than the 'knock-out' weight you speak of? Would you consider the weight-gain to be the result of a lack of self-control?"

"Probably not. I would have gained it because I set my mind to it."

"Suppose you 'set your mind' to losing weight?"

"I'd lose it."

The easy way out for Ann is to avoid her problems and do nothing. She puts up high goals for herself, worries she won't attain them, shrinks in dismay at imagined rejection, frets and feels angry and guilty and never gets around to "setting her mind" to doing the things she desperately wants to do.

Ann and others like her who suffer from lack of self-control tell themselves enough lies until the point is reached where they shout accusations at heaven, "Jesus doesn't answer my prayers! He won't change me! He doesn't love me!"

Lies.

It is not surprising when a Christian lacks self-control that his accompanying complaints are discontent, guilt, deep dissatisfaction with life, lack of self-confidence, and anger at God.

We learn many of our misbeliefs through the media.

The misbeliefs associated with poor self-control are encouraged by the media. Watch enough commercials on television and you'll begin to believe that you should have everything you want. We easily grasp the invitation to "own" something appealing or to "be" someone who has the approval of everyone around. These misbeliefs tell us *to get* what we want and get it right away (while we're still young or while the sale lasts or while it's there to get). Misbeliefs related to lack of self-control are:

1. If you want something you should have it—no matter what considerations are involved.
2. It's terrible and unjust if you have to wait to get something you want, especially if you want it very much.
3. To be uncomfortable or frustrated is terrible, intolerable. (Avoid distress at all costs.)
4. You cannot control your strong desires. They are "needs" and you can't stand it when they are not satisfied. Any time you have to spend being frustrated or ungratified is unendurable.
5. You can't stand pain or discomfort.
6. You can't stand not sleeping very well.
7. You can't stand it if others don't treat you as your doting parents did.
8. You can't stand it if circumstances aren't the way you want them to be. You may "endure" things as they are, but they are terrible and you'll let that be known.
9. You can't stand exerting yourself or having to make an effort.
10. You can't stand failure of any kind.
11. You can't fight your desires—they're much too strong for you to expect yourself to handle them.
12. You can't quit because you're too weak and besides, even though X is bad for you, it meets your need for gratification. (X stands for whatever habit happens to be the problem.)
13. You're entitled to inflict your demands upon others.

Several generations of parents have been reared on these notions and have passed them on to their children. Psychologists' and pastors' offices swell with men, women and children who are the extensions of these misbeliefs. So-called "progressive" educational methods often foster the belief that we ought to get and have what we want and like, discarding all else.

A young couple is having Sunday dinner in a restaurant with their two-year-old son. He sits on a toddler's seat placed on a chair and begins kicking the table with his foot.

"What's the matter, Sweetie?"

"He wants some bread."

Mother hands the child a chunk of bread. Two-year-old son throws it on the floor and emits a shrill scream.

"He didn't want the bread. What's the matter with him?"

"He wants your pie."

"He didn't eat his own pie. Something's upsetting him."

Father wiggles his fingers at Screaming Child. "What's the matter, Son? What is it? Here, play with your spoon."

Son hurls the spoon across the table at Father.

"*You* take care of him. Maybe he has to go potty."

Mother wiggles fingers at Screaming Child. "Want to go potty, Sweetie?"

Child screams and writhes on the seat.

"Milk. Give him some milk!"

"Here, Sweetie. Here's your milk. Come on, Sweetie, open the mouth. Attaboy, here comes the choo-choo headed for the tunnel. Choo! Cho—oh, oh, all over my dress." Mother turns helplessly to Father. "Why don't *you* do something?"

"Maybe his stomach hurts," he offers.

The interaction here is getting obvious. The child is quite capable of communicating his needs, but he has been systematically trained to believe that his parents exist primarily to spare him the trouble of coping and even of making his wants clear. Although the child could feed himself, he doesn't have to. Although he could handle some of his own problems or else ask for help, he doesn't have to. He was reinforced for yelling by the constant attention he received. Not only that, when his desires were gratified (milk, pie, spoon, potty), he learned that he could have everything he wanted and should not have to wait for it. He also learned he should never have to endure the slightest distress or discomfort.

Later in life, Screaming Child has many of these misbeliefs reinforced and strengthened as his parents continue to give him everything he expresses the least longing for. He has things done for him which he could do for himself and is never made to wait. He is also taught that to be uncomfortable is *terrible* and that above all he should *never* suffer distress.

Now what happens to Child? He grows up and discovers his friends don't comply with his demands and wants. ("Everybody hates me.") His teachers don't dote on him or make excuses for his lack of obedience. ("Nobody understands me or cares about me.") He finds that other people don't want to do for him what he can do for himself. ("The whole world is rotten!") He faces a society that requires him to comply with a certain moral code. He can't imagine denying himself something he wants, so when his peers offer him drugs, he has no reason to say no. He grows fat and sloppy in his appearance because he doesn't want to be inconvenienced or put upon. Living a chaste life is something he is not sure of; after all, one ought to get what one wants when one wants it. He believes all his fancies are vital *needs* which must always be gratified. These mistaken "needs" must be fulfilled or he's miserable. ("Life stinks. I might as well kill myself.")

Self-control? What's that?

If your teenager sounds like Screaming Child in advanced stages, don't be in a hurry to condemn yourself as a parental failure. You aren't. You have the right to make mistakes, the same as everybody else. *Behavior is learned.* Your child can learn to develop self-control in his or her life as well as learn to avoid it. It's never too late. Most of the happy, productive people we know today are that way because they worked at it. They *overcame.* Perhaps they weren't always sterling examples of self-control and dedication, but today they have attained personal gains far exceeding anything they've known before.

The devil has managed to convince millions of people that self-control is something other people have. "I just can't control myself," someone says matter-of-factly. As long as a person continues to believe this lie, it will cause itself to come true! You will find that you actually *can't* quit whatever it is you wish you didn't do; you *can't* do the thing you want so dearly to do; you *can't* resist whatever it is you know you should resist.

The can't is a lie. You *can*. Recognize the lie immediately. Look at these statements for a moment:

1. I *can't* lose weight.
2. I *can't* control my physical passions.

Remember what we said earlier: you control your feelings by your thinking. If you *think* and *tell yourself* you can't control yourself, you probably won't be able to. Can you change those sentences?

Truth

1. It's ridiculous and dumb to think I can't lose weight. Of course I can lose weight! I can say no to myself and my appetites. I can stop eating fattening foods, I can count calories, I can join Overeaters Victorious,[1] I *can* lose weight! I can do all things through Christ who strengthens me!
2. I certainly *can* control my physical passions. Jesus died on the cross to deliver me from every shred of unrighteousness, and I certainly will *not* sink to fleshly indulgence, not I. It's a lie that I have no self-control.

Once-Fail-Always-Fail Misbelief

There are many lies regarding self-control or lack of it. Some people actually *train* themselves to believe they are weak, worthless, and

1. Christian weight-loss organization with chapters all over the U.S.

inadequate. These people tell themselves, "I can't do X because I'm so helpless. I'm a failure at absolutely *every*thing."

Marsha failed to finish her two-year course of study at a church-affiliated Bible school. She didn't keep her job, either, and had to move in with her sister and her husband. She began going to singles bars where she met a young man and began a relationship with him that included sex. He vanished from her life when he learned he had gotten her pregnant. Without a job, without money, without a home except the couch in her sister's living room and pregnant, Marsha's outlook on life was grim.

Marsha taught herself to believe she was a weak person; she believed she was worthless, inadequate, and helpless. She told herself that she had piled up so many failures in her life, what else was there left for her but more failure? "Failure, failure, nothing but failure. What's the use? Why go on?"

Once-fail-always-fail is a misbelief and a lie! If you look at history, you can see what a gross lie it is! The old adage "If at first you don't succeed, try, try again" is not unsound advice. Marsha, with help, needed to learn to appreciate herself, to value herself, to see that she was indeed an important human being whom God was deeply concerned about.

From there she could learn to practice those behaviors which reinforce that truth—things that were good for her and not harmful. Eventually she realized she could return to school and finish her education. She found an apartment for herself and the baby in the same building as her sister, and developed many intimate friendships with other Christians who loved and cared for her. Marsha found her real self in Christ Jesus who never ever said, "Once-fail-always-fail."

Shirley is a woman of 36, pretty and hard-working, but distraught over her cigarette smoking. She feels trapped in a vise with no way out.

"It's no use. I've tried quitting and I can't. I always start again."

"Do you believe that when a person tries and fails at something it then becomes impossible?"

Shirley thinks for a moment. "I guess not. I applied to several schools for my teaching job. I was turned down eight times before I finally landed the job I have now."

"So that destroys your original hypothesis: 'I failed before so I always have to fail.'"

"My brother quit smoking a few years ago and he says he doesn't even think about smoking anymore. Says he doesn't even miss it."

"Had he ever tried quitting before?"

"Sure. He tried lots of times. He managed to quit for a few weeks once and then he quit for a couple of months another time. But then one day he just gave them up and hasn't lit another one since."

"Shirley, do you see the point? Your brother tried to quit several times, the same as you have. Then one day he finally *did* quit for good. It's absolutely untrue to tell yourself that past failures prove you must continue to fail."

Shirley clung to her misbelief like a child clings to a teddy bear. If she could convince herself that her habit wasn't her own fault, that she was somehow an innocent victim, she could go on smoking and not have to experience the unpleasantness of saying no to herself. The lie "I can't do something because I haven't been able to do it before" is untrue and defeating.

Jesus sets us free to be the people we were meant to be—whole, beautiful, and capable of taking His strength as ours.

> Fear thou not; for I am with thee: be not dismayed; for I am thy God: I will strengthen thee; yea, I will help thee; yea, I will uphold thee with the right hand of my righteousness.[2]

To gain self-control it is important to identify the misbeliefs in what you tell yourself. Very likely you will find that your self-control

2. Isaiah 41:10.

problems are related to the following list of lies. Never let yourself get away with mouthing one of these lies once you identify them.

Misbelief Self-Talk

- Nobody cares about me anyhow, so why should I even try to be (slim, sober, even-tempered, a non-smoker, or whatever)?
- I've had such a terrible time of life (or I've been so mistreated) I owe myself a little indulgence. So I'll go ahead and (smoke, drink, eat, steal, or whatever).
- I'm such a worthless wretch, it doesn't really matter one bit if I (destroy myself, hurt myself, get addicted to something harmful, or whatever).
- I've worked so hard and done so well, I ought to just (steal something, drink, smoke, gorge on food, or whatever).
- I *need* _____. (fill in blank)
- I can't go on without _____. (fill in blank)

Use determination and energy in arguing against each of these misbeliefs with the *truth*. The Lord is upholding you with His right hand!

The Apostle Paul says, "Blessed is the man that endureth temptation: for when he is tried, he shall receive the crown of life, which the Lord hath promised to them that love Him."[3] He tells the Corinthian Christians, "Be ye steadfast, unmovable, always abounding in the work of the Lord,"[4] and his prayer for the Christians at Ephesus was that the Lord would "grant you, according to the riches of his glory, to be strengthened with might by his Spirit in the inner man."[5]

3. James 1:12.
4. 1 Corinthians 15:58.
5. Ephesians 3:16.

Where are we strong? In the inner man, the inner *person,* in our souls where our thoughts toss and tumble waiting to create our feelings and our actions. When Paul says, "I can do all things through Christ which strengtheneth me,"[6] he gives us a dynamic lie-shredding principle to stake our very lives on. This verse is true of the entire domain of self-control behavior. Paul was writing of his own experiences as he voluntarily went without, suffered and was deprived for the sake of Christ. "I *can do* all things!" he triumphantly declared for the ages to hear.

In order to have self-control, you must actively counter your misbeliefs with the sword of the Spirit, the *truth*.

How much of our behavior is helpless? Connie, who is 65 pounds overweight, says she can't lose weight, she's *helplessly* fat. Her weakness is ice cream. We asked her to imagine she was sitting in an ice cream parlour with an enormous ice cream concoction sitting in front of her. Picking up her spoon she is about to dive into the thing when suddenly from behind her she hears someone speak.

"Drop that spoon!" he says menacingly.

She's stunned for a moment. "I said *drop* it, lady!" the voice repeats. She then feels something cold and hard against her temple. The voice is fierce. "This is a gun, lady, and if you take one bite of that ugly mess, I'll blow your head off."

Connie's reaction is immediate. "I wouldn't eat the ice cream!" she gasps.

"You mean, you wouldn't touch it?"

"I wouldn't touch it!"

So much for helplessness.

Shirley, who insists she absolutely *can't* quit smoking has a sudden change of mind when we ask her to imagine a thousand-dollar bill placed between her and a package of cigarettes. "Imagine someone saying to you, 'If you refuse to touch another cigarette for the rest of the day, this thousand dollar bill is yours.'"

6. Philippians 4:13.

94

Shirley's face brightens. "I wouldn't go near a cigarette," she laughs. We continue the story. "And then suppose at the end of the day when you've received your thousand-dollar bill, another one is placed before you and a voice says, 'Shirley, if you stay away from cigarettes for 24 more hours, you may have another thousand-dollar bill.'"

Shirley is delighted. "At this rate, I'll be rich! I wouldn't even *want* a cigarette."

"Suppose then, at the end of the 24-hour period, when you've earned yourself another thousand dollars, there's held before you a ticket for a roundtrip four-week vacation to Hawaii. You're told, "This Hawaiian vacation is yours if you refuse to smoke for three days in a row.'"

"Great!" Shirley says.

And then as a bonus, your benefactor tells you, "For every week that you do not smoke or take one puff of a cigarette, you will receive a certified check for one thousand dollars."

Shirley laughs loudly. "I see what you mean! With that kind of an offer I'd quit smoking in a huge hurry. I'd even go on an anti-smoking campaign!"

You are *not* helpless. You *do* have control over your life. You *can* do what you think may be impossible.

"I Can't Deny Myself" Misbelief

Is it so painful, really, to deny yourself something? Is it, in your mind, somehow in the same category as death and dismemberment? When you feel hungry, thirsty, sleepy, frustrated, nervous or dissatisfied, do you think you're in the pits of hell? When you are forced to endure discomfort, interruption or thwarted plans, do you tell yourself the world is coming to an end?

Sometimes it is not easy to deny yourself. It's not easy to go without something you desperately want, not easy to give up something you dearly prize, not easy to lose something you cherish. BUT sometimes for the sake of a higher, more noble life, it's necessary. Most of the time, in fact, you'll find that gaining something valuable in your life will depend on being willing to tolerate distress, anxiety, discomfort and discontent. Your greatest achievements are often won because you are willing to put up with situations which are often downright unpleasant.

You *can* deny yourself. You *can* say no to yourself. It is *not* the end of all things if you have to suffer pain. You can stand it. You really can.

Max, a brilliant graduate student in psychology, thought he was a person who would go to pieces if he had to deny himself something that was really precious to him. Then one day his wife left him and took the children with her. Max took it hard. He managed to stay in school in spite of his suffering, but his life was a wreck. He started drinking to ease the pain, which only increased his feelings of guilt and self-worthlessness.

It took a lot of effort on Max's part to finally say to himself, "Okay, so my family is gone. I'm alone, but I don't have to be lonely. I don't have to drink to ease the pain either. I *can* stand pain. It won't kill me."

Max did three dramatically life-changing things.

1. He realized he was self-destructing with his misbelief that his life and happiness depended upon another person. Happiness depends upon our relationship with Jesus. No other person should be the controlling force in our lives. "Thou shalt worship the Lord thy God, and him only shalt thou serve."[7]

2. He argued against his misbeliefs. He spoke truth to himself. ("I loved my wife and still do, but Jesus is the Lord of my life.")

3. He denied himself the temptation to wallow in self-pity and loneliness by refusing to continue drinking to ease his pain. ("I *can* stand pain!")

7. Matthew 4:10.

You *can* deny yourself.

You *can* wait for the thing you want. "In your patience possess ye your souls!"[8] Your soul is your intellect, emotions and will. How large a part patience plays in the security of your soul!

Speak the truth to yourself. Tell your soul that all is well. You *can* successfully live through inconvenience, discomfort, distress, and other negative feelings.

The "I Need" Misbelief

We get two things confused: "I need" and "I want." The word *need* implies that you cannot exist without the thing so described. An automobile *needs* oil in the crankcase, plant life *needs* water, human beings *need* oxygen; but when you tell yourself you *need* a glass of wine or a pair of blue shoes, you're not talking about need; you're talking about *want*.

All of us at one time or another have told ourselves we passionately or desperately *need* something that perhaps we really only want very much. "I *need* my favorite pillow to sleep soundly and peacefully." "I *need* my tranquilizers. If I don't take them, my nerves would fall right out of my body." "I *need* acceptance from other people in order to accept myself." "I *need* a man (or woman) to love me in order to lead a satisfying and fulfilling life."

These sentences, of course, are not true.

If you tell yourself you *need* something, or you *can't stand* something, or you *must have* something, try to stop yourself and step back for a bit of observation. Listen to those words you're telling yourself.

"I *can't stand* living in this house another moment," or, "I absolutely *must have* people around me who care about me," or, "I *can't stand* loneliness" are examples of fictionalized sentences. You can, in fact, carry on very well in spite of these annoyances and

8. Luke 21:19.

trials. You have withstood many hassles in your life and if you had to, you could survive more arduous tests than these.

By telling yourself you *can't stand* something, you increase the likelihood of avoiding or evading suffering through it. By avoiding and evading everything unpleasant in your life, you rob yourself of the rewards of endurance, patience, hope, courage and even faith. This is *not* to say that you should accept without question everything disagreeable and burdensome or ask God for trials and troubles. There are certain things that always ought to be gotten rid of, cast out, removed and avoided. You don't want to willingly hurt yourself or perform destructive acts that are against the will of God. You don't want to "accept" negativity or some woeful situation as your lot in life if the Lord clearly states in His Word that you are set free from it through the shed blood of Calvary.

The Bible says to "resist the devil, and he will flee from you,"[9] and that means we are not to blindly accept or wallow in negativity, sickness, and disaster. Jesus died on the cross to redeem our lives from sin, sickness, and destruction. "In righteousness shalt thou be established: thou shalt be far from oppression," Isaiah 54:14 tells us. That's a dear and encouraging promise.

And yet, there you are, looking for a way out of getting a job. You'd rather stay home. You don't want to face the work-a-day world, the people, the demands; you just want to stay home where you tell yourself it's cozy and safe.

But then you tell yourself there's no way out except to become and remain sick and you're too smart for that, so you fight the defeating urges and form a plan for job hunting. "People have to work in order to eat," you rightly tell yourself. "I'm no different from anyone else." When you land a job and report for work, you continue to tell yourself the truth and refuse to recite complaints and words of fear or worry. You say, "I'd rather stay home, but I'm now a working person. I'll work for the glory of God. I'll face

9. James 4:7.

this new experience and not run from it. Even though it's difficult for me, I can do it!"

You'll discover new and exciting experiences in life as well as pleasing things about yourself when *need* and *want* take their rightful place in your thinking. You'll find that you can do very nicely without everything you want, although the wants often look like needs. You can live very happily, even be a better person for enduring without some of those wants, even though the wants may seem quite respectable and reasonable to you.

Saint Paul was free from the confusion between need and want. He was able to rise above the cloying, complaining anguish of unfulfilled wants and needs. "I know both how to be abased, and I know how to abound: everywhere and in all things I am instructed both to be full and to be hungry, both to abound and suffer need. I can do all things through Christ which strengtheneth me."[10] It didn't seem to drive him to despair when things went wrong, when his plans were ruined or changed or when he suffered persecution. He then tells us confidently, *"My God shall supply all your need according to his riches in glory by Christ Jesus."*[11]

Learn the difference between need and want in your life. Write a list of your wants in a notebook. Alongside this list write down your needs. How many of your wants have you considered to be needs?

Choice—The Doorway to Joy

When you tell yourself you can't do without something or that it's terrible you have to suffer discomfort or you just can't help yourself, you're engaging in an activity called *choosing*.

Instead of saying, "I *need* _____ (fill in blank)," say the truth, which is, "I *choose* to have _____ (fill in blank)."

We are responsible for our choices.

10. Philippians 4:12.
11. Philippians 4:19.

Connie is a young college student in her Junior year. She tells herself she is "weak and easily intimidated." She talks of a domineering mother and explains that she is in college for her mother's sake.

The truth is, Connie *chooses* to let her mother be domineering. She *chooses* to go to college to please her mother. She *chooses* weak and intimidated behavior.

Too often we avoid admitting we are responsible for our own lives. We'd like to pin accountability on other people, circumstances, events, but not on ourselves and our own *choices*. How often we hear words like the following:

"If my husband would act more like the man of the house, I wouldn't be so frustrated."

(Not true. The truth is, "I *choose* to be frustrated because I *tell myself* my husband doesn't act like the man of the house.")

"If I weren't so upset and lonely, I could stop overeating."

(Not true. The truth is, "I *tell myself* I am upset and lonely and I *choose* to overeat.")

"If only I could find the right church, I'd attend every Sunday."

(Not true. The truth is, "I *tell myself* I can't find the right church and I *choose* not to attend.")

"My kids behave so terribly I've developed a temper I just can't control."

(Not true. The truth is, "I have *taught myself* to respond to my children's poor behavior with outbursts of temper. I *choose* this behavior.")

When you catch yourself in the act of telling yourself lies, be quick to label them "not true" and to replace them with the truth.

I Am Accountable for My Choices

- Admit *you* make your choices.
- Remind yourself that *you* are responsible for what you are doing.

- Prepare to accept the consequences of your behavior even if unpleasant.

An unmarried pregnant girl says, "I couldn't help myself. We were just drawn together like magnets and I couldn't say no."

The president of a respected local ministry is asked to resign because he has been stealing from the donations. "But I needed the money. I worked harder than anyone else. What else could I do?"

Both of these people are saying that someone or something else is responsible for their behavior. Both are deceived.

Self-Control Is a Choice

When you admit you are responsible for your behavior and that it's *you* who makes the choices in your life, you will be taking the first and most important step to becoming a person of self-control.

"But I didn't want to move to this town," a pretty 42-year-old woman named Dee Dee argued. "How can I tell myself that I am responsible for my actions? I didn't choose to move here. My husband made this choice, not I."

"What are your feelings about living here now?"

"I hate it. I don't want to live here. It's not my choice, that's my point. You're saying that *I* make the choices in my life. But my husband makes the choices, not I."

"Does he choose your emotions?"

"He causes them!"

"He causes them? How does he do it? Does he stand over you with a sledge hammer and shout, 'Feel this-or-that or I'll clobber you'?"

"No, he doesn't. He tells me what to *do*, though."

"And you do what he tells you to do?"

"Yes. If I didn't, he might leave me, or stop loving me or who knows what. He's a very demanding man. I've always done everything he asks, including moving here, which I didn't want to do."

"But you did it."

"Yes, I had to."

"Not quite. You *chose* to."

"*He* chose to, not I."

"But *you* chose to let him."

"But I had to."

"No, you didn't. You weighed the circumstances and then you *chose* to let your husband move you here to this city. You told yourself you had to do what he wanted to do or lose him. That's choosing."

"It's been that way our whole life together. Whatever he wants, that's what we do. I have very little say in anything."

"You choose it that way."

"No! It's just the way it is, that's all. It's *not* my choice. I'm not stupid or insignificant. I ought to have a say in things, too."

Dee Dee began at point one and studied our three checks. They are:

1. Admit you make your choices.
2. Remind yourself that you are responsible for what you are doing.
3. Prepare to accept the consequences of your behavior even if unpleasant.

We helped Dee Dee analyze what she had been telling herself. She didn't like uncovering the truth. "I came here because I wanted to work on my temper—I wanted to gain some self-control. In fact, I had hoped you'd prescribe some sort of medication."

She worked hard at facing herself and her behavior. Her gains were greater than she expected. She learned to develop skills that far surpassed the temporary effects of a pill. After several counseling sessions, she explained the three Choice Checks.

"First, I must admit I make my choices. I always thought everyone else made my choices. If I felt sad, I thought it was because of something or someone else. I never thought I was actually choosing to feel that way. My temper, the worst part, I always blamed on something else. Then the second thing, I need to remind myself I am responsible for what I am doing. Boy, that's hard. It's hard to admit I'm responsible for most of my own unhappiness. I realize that I have chosen to allow my husband to act aggressively and hurtfully to me. I also realize that I am responsible for choosing to have a bad temper."

Dee Dee is on the right track.

"Then the third Choice Check," she continued, "I remind myself of the consequences of my behavior. I am responsible; therefore I am going to have to accept it, even if unpleasant. I blamed my husband for making me move to this city. I was wrong. The truth is I *chose* to let him make this decision. And I'm choosing to feel miserable about it. The consequences for choosing to be a doormat are pretty great."

"Can you name some of these consequences?"

"Sure—my bad temper! I have been frustrated and angry at my husband, but I've chosen to avoid discussing these things with him. I have chosen to help him treat me as a doormat."

Dee Dee's communication with her husband increased and, to her surprise, he liked her honesty with him. He also liked the changes in her attitude toward herself. With the Lord's help, their marriage relationship was strengthened and enriched. "I'll never teach my husband to treat me like a doormat again," Dee Dee told us recently. "And I'll never treat him like a tyrant again, either. I found out he's really a nice guy who I never allowed to be the terrific husband he could be."

Learn to Reward Yourself

Many times the hard work it takes to develop self-control isn't worth it because there aren't enough rewards in sight.

Take Fred who wants to lose 60 pounds. It may take him six months to do it. He begins a weight-loss program and at the end of two weeks he's lost seven pounds. Instead of celebrating his victory, he's ready to throw in the towel. The thought of the 53 pounds that are left to lose is menacing; furthermore, the smell of pizza is pure ambrosia. It doesn't seem rewarding at all to painfully stick to a regimented weight-loss program, especially since gobbling up half a pizza is an extremely rewarding thought.

Where was the reward for losing seven pounds? DO reward yourself wisely and appropriately. (For the person on a weight-loss program, food can no longer serve as a reward.)

When Should You Reward Yourself?

- DO reward yourself for small successes.
- DO reward yourself when you've accomplished what you set out to accomplish.
- DO reward yourself often.
- DO reward yourself when you've exhibited self-control.
- DO reward yourself even if nobody else does.
- DO reward yourself when you've worked hard at something.
- DO not wait to reward yourself.

For some Christians the idea of rewarding themselves is nothing short of shocking. "Who *me,* reward myself? (nervous laughter). I wouldn't know *how*!"

We respond with, "Do you ever put yourself *down*?" The unhesitantly spoken answer is usually, "Yes! All the time!"

Which is more godly? Is it more Christlike to put someone down, grinding them into the dust for every fault and error committed, or is it better to bless with gentle, loving words, often and regularly?

Billy is a seven-year-old boy who bites his fingernails. His mother punishes him for this behavior, using a variety of punishments.

104

She slaps, takes away his allowance, paints his finger with a salt solution, calls him names, raises her voice in disgust, sits him in corners, threatens until she's weary—and nothing works. One day she tries rewarding him for *not* biting his fingernails. It proves far more effective than the barrage of punishers she had been using.

She begins rewarding Billy *often* and regularly for not biting his fingernails. For every hour he keeps his hands out of his mouth, she tells him sincerely and in a pleasant manner, "You lasted an hour without biting your nails. I'm proud of you. Very good. You did it." We advised her to reward him every hour at the beginning of the program and then taper off as it progressed.

When you are working on changing behavior and developing self-control, reward often for exercising the self-control you desire. Then, as the behavior improves and changes, ease off a bit, but always continue to reward.

What are rewards? First and very importantly, the *words* you say are rewards. Billy was told often and regularly how terrific it was that he didn't bite his fingernails. He won other rewards as a point system was initiated between him and his parents.

At the beginning of the week it was mutually agreed upon between Billy and his parents that he would receive a reward for earning so many points. The first week they decided together that if he earned five points, he would be allowed to stay up a half hour later than his bedtime. He chose other rewards, including having a friend over to stay all night and going to a baseball game with his dad. He responded to the reward system favorably and in a manner of a few weeks, the nail-biting problem was licked.

Billy learned that it feels good to exercise self-control. It is not punishing to have self-control. So often we shrink from self-control because we think it's so difficult to attain such a pain-inducing thing. Billy learned it isn't painful to have self-control. He felt good by the rewards he received and good about himself.

105

The punishers only served to help him hate himself and chew his nails more.

You don't control your behavior by putting yourself down or finding fault with yourself. If you lose ten pounds and gain three back, do you punish yourself for the three you gained or do you congratulate yourself for the seven you lost? More than likely you'll punish yourself first.

God doesn't spend all His time punishing. In fact, He loved us so much He sent us His Son, Jesus Christ, to take the punishment for our sins from us! Forgiveness is one of our most precious gifts. To refuse forgiveness is an insult to the work done on the cross. God is love!

Picture the Lord saying to you, "Well done, thou good and faithful servant" when you exercise self-control or when you have conquered a misbelief. Say "Well done!" out loud to yourself. Smile at yourself! You deserve it!

Stop dwelling on negatives, stop making lists of your failures. Stop saying hurtful words to yourself, stop calling yourself names, stop putting yourself down for being such a lousy Christian. Stop telling yourself you don't deserve any blessings from God. Stop piling on the guilt and condemnation.

Jesus died on the cross for you to take the guilt and condemnation from you. If you have sincerely repented from the sins in your life, go on from there. Stop dwelling on them. Pick yourself up and carry on.

Naturally, don't reward yourself for failure or pretend you're something greater than you are, but at the same time don't go on punishing yourself for every mishap in your life. Much better results will be achieved by rewarding yourself for doing well than punishing yourself for every nonsuccess.

There is therefore now no condemnation to them which are in Christ Jesus, who walk not after the flesh, but after the Spirit.[12]

12. Romans 8:1.

Who Did It? Jesus or I?

One misbelief that prevents some Christians from rewarding themselves for real accomplishment is the notion that they didn't do it—it was the Lord who did it. This is a misbelief because it teaches an impossible and unscriptural psychology.

It *is* true that out of our old sinful selves no good thing can flow. It *is* true that without the Holy Spirit we can do nothing (good). But it is *also* true that with the Holy Spirit at work within, *we* do the good.

You cannot have faith without the gift of faith, but the faith you have is yours. *You* do the believing. It is not the Holy Spirit's faith, but *your* faith which saved you. When you gain a small victory over a bad habit, you might want to say you had nothing to do with it. But you had plenty to do with it. Through Him, *you* did it.

It's true that you cannot accomplish anything or gain victory over sin and self without Him ("Without me ye can do nothing,"[13] He tells us)—but we must realize we live our lives *through, in,* and *with* Him. When you were born again into Christ, you didn't move out of your body. You are still there, only now you are a new person with a new godly nature. ("Old things are passed away; behold, all things are become new."[14])

Saint Paul said, "I am crucified with Christ: nevertheless I live; yet not I, but Christ liveth in me: and the life which I now live in the flesh I live by the faith of the Son of God, who loved me, and gave himself for me."[15] By this Paul is saying he has been crucified (by choice) and the self who ruled his life previously has been put to death. When Jesus went to the cross on our behalf He gave us that great possibility of being *saved from ourselves* by allowing His life to enter and transform ours.

We as Christians have the opportunity of making a commitment so all-inclusive and permanent that temptation to selfishness

13. John 15:5.
14. 2 Corinthians 5:17.
15. Galatians 2:20.

and sin will not have the binding hold on us as in the former days. Christ, living within us by His Holy Spirit, will have the chief position in our lives! This thundering truth is the very purpose for writing this book. We are showing you in a practical and tangible way how you can cooperate with the provision Christ has made for you, enabling you to crucify the "flesh with its affections and lusts" which previously enslaved you, and release the new, born-again Christian, Spirit-indwelled *victorious* you!

Praise God for your victories! Because of Christ, you can gain the victory! Reward yourself with kind and soothing words for your obedience to Him.

How to Reward Yourself

- DO reward yourself by telling yourself "Well done!" or "Good job!" or other words of honest appreciation.

- DO reward yourself with activities you enjoy. Examples: "When I finish cleaning the oven and scouring the appliances, I am going to reward myself with words of appreciation and then I am going to take a long, luxurious bubble bath." Or, "Now that I've lost two and a half pounds, I am going to reward myself by setting aside an evening to relax in my favorite chair and read without any interruptions."

- DO reward yourself, as you can, with token awards. Examples: "I've done such a good job of building these shelves, I'm going to buy myself a new set of screwdrivers." "I have improved nearly 100% getting places on time and I'm pleased with myself. I'm going to reward myself by getting my watch fixed."

- DO reward yourself by helping others learn what you've learned.

- DO reward yourself for spiritual victories by enjoying the feelings of joy and confidence which come through the Holy Spirit.

Disconnect the Triggers That Set off the Bomb

List your trigger situations. What triggers the behavior you don't want? Then begin cutting the triggers one at a time, gradually reducing the number of situations in which you allow the behavior to occur. For example, if you're trying to quit smoking, eliminate some of the triggers that make you think of having cigarettes. They might be:

1. Sitting at the table after a meal with a cup of coffee.
2. Sitting in the smoking section of restaurants.
3. Taking a soft-drink break.

After gradually eliminating the triggers, then imagine yourself in these situations doing these same activities *without* cigarettes, Prepare yourself for not smoking.

Finally, after you have disconnected all the triggers but one, you can either remove the behavior from your life entirely, or you can keep practicing the behavior, linking it only to that little trigger.

You can do yourself a big favor by getting rid of all the triggers that set off the bomb. Don't allow yourself to be in places of temptation with your girlfriend or boyfriend if you're trying to maintain mastery over the sin of lust. Don't keep candy in your cupboards if you're trying to lose weight. Don't carry your credit cards when you go shopping if you're a compulsive buyer.

If you disconnect the linkage between the trigger and the firing pin of a gun, the weapon won't fire. Most behaviors have triggers or situations which cause the behaviors to occur. Recognize yours.

You Can Be a Self-Controlled Person!

He feedeth on ashes: a deceived heart hath turned him aside, that he cannot deliver his soul, nor say, Is there not a lie in my right hand?[16]

16. Isaiah 44:20.

The most important thing you can do to increase your self-control is to identify the misbeliefs in the words you tell yourself. Then argue against those misbeliefs. Never let yourself get away with misbelief talk. Use determination and energy in arguing and refusing each misbelief with the truth.

You can be self-controlled in every area of your life. People who exercise self-control have discovered a major key to living fulfilled lives.

Laziness, apathy and lethargy, and avoiding responsibility are not inroads to happiness and the fulfilled life. It is not surprising that when a person complains of lack of self-control the accompanying complaints are discontent, guilt, deep dissatisfaction with life, and a lack of self-confidence.

Self-control, a fruit of the Spirit, will become a part of your life as you diligently cultivate it, as you reject discouragement, and as you teach yourself to reward yourself for your successes. "Let us not be weary in well doing: for in due season we shall reap, if we faint not," Paul tells us in Galatians 6:9. Allow the Holy Spirit to help you. With God, nothing is impossible. Sometimes things may seem difficult, but with the Lord as your helper, strength and guide, it's not impossible.

You can shout to the whole world, " 'Greater is he [the Holy Spirit] that is in me than he [the devil who tempts me to sin] that is in the world.'[17] Therefore, I can be and am a self-controlled person!"

17. 1 John 4:4.

8

Misbelief in Self-Hate

Arnie is 29 years old. He suffers with intense anxiety attacks. He is nervous, tense and often feels depressed for seemingly "no reason at all." At home he frequently has outbursts of temper where he flies into a rage over small things. Outside the home he is usually as gentle as a lamb; on the job he has been called Mr. Nice Guy, and in his church he has been known as the person who will do anything for anyone, Good Old Arnie.

Arnie has been people-pleasing for years. He has done what he has felt people expected of him. The major decisions in his life such as education, marriage, and a career choice were made largely through the influence of others. When he had the approval of others, he felt he was doing right. He felt worthwhile when he was approved of and pleasing others.

When he was a teenager, it was very important to him that he be accepted as one of the crowd. He worked hard at being popular, cool and "with it." He was well liked by the other teenagers and had many friends. He was also popular with the girls.

There wasn't anything unusual about his behavior because being liked and fitting in with the group is important to all teenagers. It's at this stage of life that fear of social rejection is greater than the child's fear of being hurt or dying. Arnie was an average teen, then, you might say, because he pursued being liked and approved of by others.

But then Arnie graduated from high school. Most of his friends went to the State University, so Arnie went to the State University. Drugs and booze were now the big thing. Arnie followed the crowd. His friends got high, so Arnie got high; his friends had loose morals, so Arnie had loose morals. His parents worried about him because he was missing school. Everybody's pal, Arnie, began to flunk out after two semesters.

He managed to stay in school on probation, but many of his friends were dropping out. Some of them were getting married. Arnie began to date a girl who didn't smoke or drink, which pleased his parents, and they encouraged the relationship. Arnie wasn't sure he wanted to be serious with her and about the time he was making a decision to break up, she disclosed the news that she was pregnant.

Arnie married the girl, as was expected of him. He dropped out of school entirely, abandoning the idea of evening classes, and took a job in his father-in-law's company, where he works to this day.

Three years ago Arnie and his wife had a conversion experience and they gave their hearts to Jesus Christ. Their two children are Christians and love the Lord, too, and they are an active family in their church. But Arnie is unhappy.

He can't understand what's wrong. When he became a Christian he gave his testimony many times telling what the Lord had saved him from. He told about his past life in drugs and loose living and how glad he was to be a new person in Christ, washed in the blood of Jesus. The Christians in his church were thrilled to see what the power of God could do in a person. So how come he was so miserable?

"What's wrong with me?" Arnie asked. "I'm supposed to be filled with joy. I'm a Christian!" He feels he has to control his negative feelings because that's what other people expect him to do. He feels that if he allows his true feelings to emerge, he will be judged and condemned for them. He has given testimony to how much better his life is now that he is a Christian, and he doesn't want to look like a hypocrite by exposing his unhappy and depressed feelings.

Arnie has taught himself over the years that he has to meet the expectations of the people around him. At church he does and says exactly what he thinks other people expect. He dresses, talks, walks and does as he thinks the congregation and pastor would expect of a fine upstanding Christian man.

At the job he does exactly as expected of him, also. He gets along with his father-in-law because he has his approval. The truth of it is, he doesn't really like the work he does, but it's more important to him to be accepted and liked than it is to be doing something he wants to do and likes to do. In fact, he gets the two confused. He associates being approved of with being happy.

At home he thinks his wife has certain expectations of him and so he fulfills those. The house, the car, the furniture, the appliances, even the vacations—he provides acceptably and agreeably. Everybody's satisfied, everything is fine and dandy. What's wrong?

For most of his life Arnie has not allowed himself to think of himself and his own needs as very important. He brought these beliefs into his Christian life, and because they're not always easy to detect, he was able to carry on as his usual Terrific Guy self without being found out, least of all to himself. After all, isn't the Christian supposed to honor his neighbor higher than himself?

You can't honor your neighbor as he ought to be if you don't give any honor to yourself. At best your feelings are neurotic and self-debasing. God does not want us debased. He wants us healthy and sound of mind.

113

The self-debaser flatters others to get their approval. If others don't approve of him, he feels worthless. His own good opinions of himself don't mean a thing. Other people's opinions are what count.

Arnie doesn't consider his own needs and feelings as important. As long as he is pleasing others, he feels his life is going along okay. As long as others like him and approve of him, he feels things are fine. But now he is finding out things aren't okay or fine at all.

Almost 30 years old, he is still living the anxieties of an adolescent. Because of it he can't really love others.

Some of Arnie's misbeliefs are:

1. The way to be liked by others is to be what others want me to be and to do what is most pleasing to them.

2. It is more Christian to please other people than to please myself.

3. Other people have every right to judge my actions.

4. It is wrong and unChristian to think of my own needs, or to consider my own needs important, compared to the wants of others.

5. It is wrong not to be willing to forget my own wants to please friends and family when they want me to.

6. Pleasing others is an insurance policy which guarantees that people will be nice to me in return. When I am in great need they will forget their own needs to help me.

7. When others are displeased with me, I cannot enjoy one moment's peace or happiness.

8. Approval from everyone else is essential to my feeling of well-being and peace of mind, since God doesn't want me to be happy unless everyone else is approving of me.

9. Being what other people want me to be is the only way to be liked.

10. Pleasing others and doing what they expect of me is the only way to win friends.

If you believe any of the above, you're believing lies.

In 1 Samuel 18:1, we read that the soul of Jonathan was knit with the soul of David and that Jonathan loved David "as his own soul." When the true knitting of souls in sincere friendship occurs, it is not lopsided or out of kilter; it is not living to please and gain approval of another. It is *a joint* relationship, a knitting of souls. Jesus taught that we are to love others *as* ourselves.[1]

"Thou shalt love thy neighbor as thyself" means to consider the needs of others as *equally* important with your own, to value others' opinions equally with your own, to respect the rights of others as much as your own rights. It means that other people are not less important than you and they are also not more important than you. This thinking takes effort. Sometimes it is easier and more comfortable to degrade yourself and believe that others' opinions of you are more important than your own. Arnie was a person who relied on other people for his own feelings of self-worth. If someone didn't like or approve of him, he thought it meant something was wrong with him.

The Scriptures teach us two important truths about our self-worth.

1. Our life, including our opinions, feelings, wants and needs, is not less valuable or important than anyone else's and
2. Our life, including our opinions, feelings, wants and needs, is not more valuable or important than anyone else's.

When you gaze out the tour bus window at the hungry illiterate peasants of an underprivileged country, remember your needs are not more important than theirs. And at the same time, the needs of others are not more important than yours.

When Jesus said, "Greater love hath no man than this, that a man lay down his life for his friends,"[2] He prepared the way for

1. Matthew 19:19.
2. John 15:13.

us to be able to love ourselves in the purest sense. Condemnation, guilt, despair, self-degradation, shame and self-hate have all been nailed to the cross in His body. By His taking our sin on the cross with Him, we are set free to live healthy and abundant lives with wholesome, pure, swept-clean attitudes. When our lives are really beautiful in the eyes of God, they are pure and clean in the holiest sense. When do we please Him but when we are right before Him, living as He has shown us to live? If we lay down our lives out of guilt and self-hate, we are not fulfilling the very meaning of the above verse, "Greater *love* hath no man . . ."

> Hereby perceive we the love of God *[notice:* the love *of God]*, because he laid down his life for us: and we ought to lay down our lives for the brethren.[3]

What good does it do God or anybody else if you lay down your life because you can't stand yourself? Jesus died on the cross for you, and to despise yourself is to insult Him. We despise *sin*, not people.

We ought not to forget that our lives are made up of such things as honesty, courage, sense of humor and most precious of all possessions, *wisdom*. These we can give to one another as loving, unselfish gifts.

Elaine is a woman who is a lot like Arnie, but whereas Arnie reacts to his misbeliefs with depressed and woebegone feelings, Elaine reacts with rage. She is a woman of 35 who looks more like 45. Haggard, worn, droopy, she rarely laughs or relaxes. She has believed for years that she has to sublimate her own wishes for everyone else's and she's tired of it. She says she has been a doormat for her family and friends; even strangers have pushed her around. "The Bible says to give and so I give," she says angrily. She's upset because she feels guilty about feeling angry. Her words snap with bitterness and resentment.

3. 1 John 3:16.

"Nobody ever does anything for *me*," she says; "and no matter what I do, they don't have any respect for me. I'm just a *thing* for people to *use*, that's all. I shouldn't be angry, I know. I suppose it's just selfishness on my part. I just don't know what to do about it. I'm probably a lousy Christian, but I can't help it."

The Word of God tells us to fellowship with one another, to love one another, to give and share and forgive; to be kind, generous and tender-hearted. Indeed, the Lord tells us to bear our lives toward one another; but not in a downgrading way and not for self-denunciating motives; not to become slaves to other people's whims, and not for *people-pleasing* motives. All of these are self-hate indicators. Elaine's "doormat" really *was* selfishness in different attire.

"What makes you think you're a lousy Christian?" we asked Elaine.

"A Christian shouldn't get so mad. I'm supposed to be above it all. I'm supposed to just give-give-give and not ask for anything in return; I know all that self-denying stuff."

She slaps the chair with the palm of her hand. "I bend over backwards for my friends, for my kids, for my husband. And not only that, I've got a very demanding mother. She still has me driving her all over town because she doesn't drive. I've got six kids and I'm in the middle of eating dinner and she calls and expects me to drop everything and come running for her."

"And you do?"

"Of course! She'd probably have heart failure if I didn't. She expects it of me. That's how everybody treats me. I'm just a *thing* to be *used*."

"You've said that before. What does that mean—a thing to be used?"

"I'm a nothing. N-o-t-h-i-n-g!"

"Says who?"

"Says everybody! Look how they treat me!"

"Does everybody else decide your importance?"

"What do you mean by that?"

"Well, why is it you think everybody else decides whether or not you are an important and worthwhile person? What happened to your own opinion of yourself?"

"My opinion of myself stinks."

"If your opinion of yourself stinks, how do you expect other people to treat you with consideration and respect?"

"I don't know and I don't care. All I know is that the whole world can go take a flying jump."

You can hear the bitterness in Elaine's words. She has worked all her life for approval and love and now sees it hasn't paid off. For all her years of sacrifice she sees nothing but dust and emptiness. She has made herself a victim of other people's whims in order to please them and earn their approval and love. If someone else would tell her she was a giving and dear person, she might feel worthwhile for a moment or two, although she would disagree. When no words of acceptance and approval are forth-coming, she feels desperate and hopeless. She really believes she is nothing but a *thing* to be *used*.

The people Elaine gave the most to, such as her mother who thought it not presumptuous to call her at any hour of the day to be driven somewhere, gave her the least returns in acceptance and love. Elaine believed she had to *earn* her worth and *earn* the right to be loved and so the harder she worked, the worse she felt.

You have more than likely already labeled many of Elaine's misbeliefs.

- If I don't give, give, give, I'm not a good Christian. (Elaine wasn't really *giving;* she was *doing* things to *get* something for herself.)
- I'm supposed to be appreciated for all I give. (True giving doesn't even need acknowledgment.)
- My self-worth depends on the opinions of other people.

- Love is something you *earn* and *work* for.
- Respect is something you *earn* and *work* for.
- If I don't do what other people want and expect me to do, they won't like me.
- If I don't do what other people want me to do, I don't *deserve* their approval or friendship.
- Other people have the right to ask anything they want of me in order that I won't offend anyone.
- If others do not tell me I am a good person, then I must not be.
- If someone does not like me, there is something wrong with me.
- If someone is angry with me, it must be my fault.
- It's my duty to make everybody happy and comfortable.
- It's my duty to work my fingers to the bone for my family. If I don't, they might reject me.

Elaine thought her problem was not being able to give *enough*. Some of the additional lies she told herself were:

- Rejection and not being liked are terrible.
- In spite of how hard I work to earn approval, some people still don't like me and reject me; therefore I am terrible.
- It's terrible to be angry,
- I am angry; therefore I am terrible.
- It's terrible to be a *thing* other people *use.*
- I am a thing other people use; therefore I am terrible.
- It's terrible not to be able to conquer my bad feelings.
- I can't conquer my bad feelings. Therefore I am terrible.

Elaine had to learn, first, that she was important and valuable because *God* says so, and secondly, because she agrees with God. People do not respond favorably to someone who hates himself/

herself. Elaine wanted respect from her friends and family, but she had no respect for herself, realizing her own underlying selfish motives. She depended upon others to prove whether she was worth anything or not. Other people did not show her the respect she tried so feverishly to earn.

There is a difference between self-respect and selfishness. The person who truly respects himself is genuinely interested in others, giving of himself without fear. He may even find on occasion that the most loving thing he can do for another person is to say no to him. A selfish person, however, is greedy, fearful, and manipulative. Elaine had many of these behavior patterns and she was forced to face them. Usually the tendencies toward greed and selfishness in an individual motivate him to live for the approval of others, always striving to satisfy an insatiable need within himself.

Both Elaine and Arnie had to learn that a Christian is an important person, special, and loved, *period*. Their self-worth, as well as yours and ours, does not depend upon others' opinions, but upon God's declaration. We are God's temples on earth—real, honest living temples where the King of Power lives and makes His home. "Know ye not that ye are the temple of God, and that the Spirit of God dwelleth in you?"[4] A most godly thing for you to do is to have respect and love for yourself.

"*Godly?*" asked Elaine. "How can it be godly to love myself? I thought that was vanity." In order to love yourself, you must be a lovely person; and that happens when a person allows himself to be crucified to sin (selfishness) and come alive to God through the power of the Holy Spirit.

Vanity is not accompanied by contentment and peace. You can recognize your own godly motives by the contentment and peace that surround them. You won't be living in strife if your motives are godly.

4. 1 Corinthians 3:16.

Godliness and Contentment

"Godliness with contentment is great gain"[5] is a verse for the self-hater. When you are doing what the Lord is showing you to do, you can experience real contentment even through hard times and in hard tasks. A sign of a people-pleaser is a lack of contentment. When the going gets rough, the people-pleaser starts to find fault and complain. Eventually, if things continue to go wrong, he becomes enraged.

Elaine cried in exasperation, "The whole *world* can go take a flying jump!" Arnie threw temper tantrums at home and yelled at the children for the slightest mistake.

Loving yourself is to be content with yourself whether or not other people approve of you. With God's approval, you no longer are compelled to *earn* love and acceptance. You're free to be you—for better or worse.

Loving yourself is not selfish. You don't become an aggressive bully who demands his/her own way from all those around. Far from it!

Loving yourself is seen in your self-respect, your wisdom, and in your integrity. You see the nobleness of humility. You love and respect yourself because you belong to the Lord Jesus. Your life is His and the Holy Spirit lives in the temple of your being. The Lord has wonderfully created and designed you, as He has those around you. You love yourself; therefore you can love others.

Arnie's moment of truth came when we asked him to seriously answer the question, "How important is it to you that you always please and gain the approval of others?"

He was stunned to discover how much of his life was lived solely to please and impress other people. As of this writing, he has made many changes in his life and learned to respect himself for who he is. Elaine, also, has made changes in her life. By changing her attitudes and the misbeliefs we listed, she has found that she can have the respect of others just by being herself.

5. 1 Timothy 6:6.

When you stop striving to get the approval of others, you'll gain it without trying. When you like yourself, others will like you, too. When you accept yourself, others will accept you, too. And if they do not approve, accept or like you? What happens?

You discover you can live with it. It's not *terrible* not to be liked!

Tell yourself these words of truth instead of the misbeliefs you may be harboring in your own belief system. *It's all right if everybody doesn't like me!*

Truth

- It is *not* necessary to be liked by everyone.
- I do not have to earn anyone's approval or acceptance.
- I am a child of God. I am deeply loved by Him, I have been forgiven by Him; therefore I am acceptable. I accept myself.
- My needs and wants are as important as other people's.
- Rejection is *not* terrible. It may be a bit unpleasant, but it's not terrible.
- Not being approved of or accepted is *not* terrible. It may not be desirable, but it's not terrible.
- If somebody doesn't like me, I can live with it. I don't have to work feverishly to get him/her to like me.
- I can conquer my bad feelings by distinguishing the truth from misbelief.
- It is a misbelief that I must please others and be approved of by them.
- Jesus died on the cross for me so that I can be free from the misbelief that other people decide my value.

Meditate on the following:

1. Pleasing others is a principle which may be directly opposed to the basic rule of the Christian's life: to *please God*. God's will for

you may be at variance with others' claims, demands and whims. God's will for Jesus, for example, was contrary to the demands of the multitude who wanted to make Him king after He fed 5,000 people with the little boy's meager lunch (John 6). The disciples objected strenuously to the will of God for Jesus when He foretold His coming crucifixion and death, also. Peter was upset at the news. "May it never be!" he said. Jesus answered, "Get thee behind me, Satan."

2. Frequently, God's will for you will require that you consider your own needs first and set aside the wishes of others. There were times when Jesus put His own needs for rest and food ahead of ministering to others. If you try to neglect yourself and your own needs (unless you are under direct instructions from the Lord), you will court spiritual and psychological troubles. Being cruel to yourself is not necessarily holy. Jesus did your penance for you on the cross. You're free now to live in love, receiving as well as giving.

3. In making judgments about what you should do, it is too simplistic to base priority on the rule: Whatever pleases others must be right. True, the critical needs of another human being will very likely often be given precedence over your own plans and less critical needs, and at times even over your own crucial needs. If you encounter a dying man at your doorstep when you are on the way to a prayer meeting, you would probably give up the prayer meeting to help the man. But notice, the question to answer is not: Is someone else expecting it of me? but rather, *Is God directing me to do it?*

4. If you live to please others, any negative feedback, criticism or displeasure will tend to ruin you. It will disturb you terribly to think that others are not perfectly happy with you. You must learn to take criticism and handle it as a "very small thing," to quote Saint Paul who knew it was the Lord who was the true judge.[6]

5. Even if everyone disliked you and disapproved of you, you could still survive. Jesus did. Many others have managed to live

6. 1 Corinthians 4:3, 4.

through large amounts of disapproval by others. If you are willing to take God at His Word, "I will not leave you nor forsake you!"[7]—there is no reason to believe that you will collapse or disintegrate when others disapprove of you. Of course, the displeasure of others is often unpleasant for us to tolerate, and it may be very difficult to endure, especially when those who are important to us do not approve of us. Nevertheless, if we have to, we can stand it. And most of the time disapproval by others is short-lived and restricted. It is very unlikely that we will encounter a circumstance where absolutely *everyone* will dislike us and disapprove of us.

Much of our social custom teaches us to manipulate for acceptance and approval. If you invite the Joneses to dinner, they'll invite you in return. If you help the Joneses paint their house, they may help paint yours; if you take the Joneses to lunch they may take you to lunch; it's the "if you scratch my back, I'll scratch yours" philosophy.

Godly motives are higher. They say, "I care about you and I want you to care about me. I will not demand or insist you care about me, however, and I will not strive to earn your approval, affection or friendship. I care about you and I also care about me because Jesus died for each of us."

Godly motives say, "You are important and so am I. Jesus loves us—and He loves us equally."

You can be released forever from the grip of self-hate when you freely and fully know the approval of God is far more precious than the approval of people.

7. Hebrews 13:5.

9

Misbelief in Fear of Change

"I'm the way I am. I'll never change," says Lila, a 34-year-old elementary schoolteacher. Exasperated at the end of the day, she often makes statements such as, "My third-graders make me furious. I probably shouldn't have been a teacher with my low tolerance level." She had been raising her voice in class, losing patience, and at times had taken a child by the shoulders and harshly shaken him. As a result she is deeply distressed and frustrated at her lack of self-control.

Joe is 25 and a bright engineering student in graduate school. His fiancée is concerned about his frequent outbursts of anger and tries to talk to him about the problem. He shrugs and tells her, "I'm the way I am. Take it or leave it, I'm me. So I've got a rotten temper and when something makes me mad, I show it. I can't help it." He concludes the discussion with, "I take after my dad. He has a rotten temper and so do I."

Shirley is a patient at the Center for Christian Psychological Services and is seeing her therapist for the third time. She sits stiffly upright in the comfortable armchair. There are tears burning the edges of her eyes. She is 29 years old, overweight and her appearance says, *I don't care about me*. She admits between tears that she is afraid she's losing her husband. He has been accusing her of being a slob and nagging her to lose weight. She thinks he's seeing another woman.

"I'm fat and I know it," she cries. "He doesn't have to remind me. If I were slim, things would be different. He'd never look around at other women."

She pauses to blow her nose. "I *can't* lose weight. He likes me to cook him fattening, rich foods. He is thin and can eat all those foods that I'm not supposed to. How am I supposed to lose weight when he's eating all the things I love? It's impossible."

Lila, Joe, and Shirley share in common several misbeliefs. Lila believes it is her third-grade class that makes her feel anger, not realizing that she alone allows herself to be angry. She believes her anger is a permanent characteristic of her personality, which is untrue. Jesus died on the cross to free us from our sins as well as permanent "low tolerance thresholds." Lila cuts off possibilities for constructive alteration in her life and insults the work the Lord did on the cross for her.

Joe is a person who believes it's perfectly permissible to indulge in temper tantrums whenever he pleases because, after all, his father has temper tantrums, too. He tells himself and other people, "I'm me. Take it or leave it." He means, "I can't (or won't) change."

Shirley puts the blame for her overweight and slovenly appearance on her husband. She tells herself she isn't responsible in the least for her life—he is. Now she fears he's going to stray and she's terrified she might have to act responsibly and exert herself with discipline and direction.

Lila, Joe, and Shirley believe the fault of the unsatisfactory conditions or circumstances in their lives is *outside of their own control*. They have avoided taking responsibility for their feelings and actions. They also believe they can't change.

Sometimes it's not hard to think you're a victim of circumstances. Look around you for a moment. How many times in your day or week do you put the responsibility for your feelings and actions on some-thing or someone outside of your control? Have you ever tripped over your own foot and then twirled around you as if there were a loose board in the floor or a crevice in the earth that was to blame? Whose fault is it when you burn your mouth on the hot drink? Why do you glare at the cup? How many times have you accused someone *else* of *making* you angry, or *making* you frustrated, or *making* you unhappy?

Nobody *else* makes you experience these attitudes. You do it yourself. Nobody forces you to feel, think, and behave as you do. A man in his early thirties said, "I do drugs because all my friends do drugs. I was arrested for dealing and now I'm facing a jail term. But it's not my fault I got caught." Stop blaming other people for your problems and your sins. Nobody *makes* you do anything. Nobody makes you sin. You do it all by yourself.

Naturally, circumstances and people around you will have some influence in your life; for example, you won't feel your best if you've got the flu, or if you're married to a person who throws pineapples at you every time you clear your throat. You're going to respond differently than if he were throwing kisses. BUT what we are dem-onstrating to you through this book is that *you* decide *how* you will respond to events and circumstances in your life by how you *believe*. You decide if you want to do as your friends do, whether it's joining a club, taking drugs, or whatever.

It would be untrue to say, "The reason I'm so grouchy is because I've got the flu." The *truth* would be, "I am making myself grouchy and allowing myself to act in a grouchy way. The flu causes me to experience unpleasant sensations in my body and emotions, but I do not have to react in such a way as to make life difficult for oth-ers. I could decide to be cheerful if I chose to."

The misbelief in this disagreeable behavior is, "As long as I'm ill it's permissible to act unpleasantly and selfishly."

Too often we blame others for our feelings. Imagine you are a man married to a woman who throws pineapples at you. It would be untrue if you were to say, "I'm a nervous wreck because my wife throws pineapples at me."

The misbelief is: "My peace of mind depends upon the behavior of others, and I can do nothing about their behavior." The *truth* would be, "It is unpleasant to have pineapples thrown at me and I don't like it one bit"; furthermore, "if I allow her to continue the behavior, I will only be teaching her that it is okay for her to abuse me in this way."

When you hear yourself reciting misbeliefs to yourself, a buzzer ought to go off in your mind followed by the words, "Not true!" *The truth is, I'm responsible for my feelings and actions! Nobody and nothing else is. I am.*

Here are some misbeliefs which should activate your buzzer:

"I'm the way I am because I was born that way."

"If I had a better education, I'd be better liked."

"If I were like so-and-so I'd be a happier person."

"If I were better looking, I'd be a happier person."

"It's not what you know; it's who you know. That's why I'm not more successful."

"Children make me edgy and tense."

"My in-laws make me edgy and tense."

"You make me mad."

"If only I were younger, then I'd have more energy and I'd be happier."

"If only I lived in a better neighborhood. Then I'd be happy."

"This house depresses me."

"I know I should change but I just can't."

"The reason I drink is because of the pressures I face every day."

"The reason I curse is because everyone at the office curses."

"The reason I steal is because my boss is too cheap to give me the raise I deserve."

If you believe any of these inventions, you are identifying the wrong culprit. Your most fierce enemy is not outside yourself, but within. For the most part, you *learned* how to think, feel and act the way you do; therefore, if need be, *you can unlearn it.*

Are you blaming other people for some unhappiness you are suffering? Is there a troublesome situation in your life which you are allowing and thereby telling yourself is the cause of your stress?

Unlearn Your Old Way of Thinking

1. Realize that joy comes from your relationship to God and His unchanging faithfulness.

You don't need to live in perfect circumstances to be happy. You don't even have to be loved and appreciated by others in order to be happy. It's pleasant to be loved and appreciated, but not *vital* to your happiness.

The Bible tells how two men of God, Paul and Silas, were brought before Roman authorities at Philippi and beaten with rods and then thrown into jail. Bleeding and pain-wracked, they lay on the cold, dark prison floor with their feet fastened in stocks. But did Paul and Silas moan and complain, "If it weren't for the cruelty of the unbelievers, we wouldn't be wounded and bleeding and we'd be happy!"?

Did they howl in agony, "Those unjust, unfair, rotten heathen! Look what they've done to us!"? Suppose it were you or I lying on that unfriendly dirt floor with rats and insects skittering across our own blood in the dirt? Would we grieve, "This life as an evangelist stinks. It's nothing but abuse and suffering! Who needs it? Nobody cares, nobody helps, nobody wants to hear the Good News. Here I am, half dead and for what? Who knows if God even cares?"

Paul and Silas had strong beliefs that transcended circumstances, events, people, feelings; it even transcended pain. That belief was in the person, power, and presence of Jesus Christ. They believed their suffering wasn't as important as the message they carried.

So at midnight, instead of writhing and groaning in pain, they prayed and sang praises unto God. They did not complain, blaming someone else for their physical agony, and they did not agonize in silence, biting their lips and despairing that God allowed such an awful fate to befall them. Instead, they sang so loudly their voices were heard throughout the prison! And not only that, God heard them and opened the prison doors for them. Their happiness came from the belief in Jesus Christ within them and not from circumstances around them.

2. *You are in control of your happiness or unhappiness.*

You make the choice to be happy. *You* make the choice to think true thoughts about yourself and others. You are the one who chooses not to blame the rest of the world for your misfortunes; *you* choose to stop excusing your improper behavior and putting the blame for your actions elsewhere. You face yourself as you are right now, taking responsibility for your thoughts, feelings, and attitudes.

People don't make you angry, sad, sick, etc. You *allow* yourself to be angry, sad, sick or whatever the negative feeling is you are experiencing. Indulging in temper tantrums is learned behavior. You learned to throw temper tantrums and you can learn to stop. It is utter fakery to believe you cannot change your behavior.

	MISBELIEF	TRUTH
1.	The things you say to me make me angry!	I make myself angry at the things you say to me.
2.	It makes me very upset when you don't have dinner ready on time.	I upset myself when dinner isn't ready when I expect it.

You are not so much disturbed by things—external events—but by the view you take of them—the beliefs you have about them.

A Christian should never live a life dominated by outside circumstances. Much of our suffering is because we lack the skills necessary for sound and happy living as the Bible teaches: "I have learned in whatsoever state I am in therewith to be content." We continue to believe love and joy depend upon other people, circumstances, events, material blessings, success, achievement, abilities, and other such things.

You may be unhappy because you are looking in the wrong place for happiness.

You Can Change!

Being "content in whatever circumstances I am" does not necessarily mean suffering in silence. It means to understand that your joy does not lie in your circumstances, but joy comes from within you. With Jesus Christ living within you by the power of His Holy Spirit, you are able to realize joy and contentment in *Him*.

Many circumstances are within your power to change. Suffering in silence is no sign of virtue (although there are times when the Lord leads us to hush and wait on Him even though we are going through a particularly difficult period). But oftentimes it can be more destructive to silently pine away in anguish than it is to rise up and do something about it. Many people do nothing about their suffering because they are afraid to. Fear of other people may be the major reason.

Shirley tells herself, "My husband may get angry with me if I tell him I want him to stop bringing home ice cream and pizza when I'm trying to diet. Therefore, I won't say anything and I'll eat the stuff. Sure, I'll continue to gain weight, but it's not my fault. It's his."

Lila says, "I don't dare let the other teachers see I'm having problems with my class. They'll think I'm an inferior teacher."

Joe's dad believes a man should be gruff and hostile, especially toward women, so rather than argue or reason for himself, Joe imitates his dad. It's less risky than making his own decisions and receiving the consequences of ridicule his dad would regale him with.

131

Not only do you change your behavior, you change your attitudes about the consequences of your change. Shirley can stop eating the pizza and ice cream her husband brings home when she realizes she is the only person on earth with the power to make herself fat or thin. If her husband disapproves of her change, Shirley can handle it by preparing herself for negative consequences.

She tells herself, "It's okay for my husband to disapprove of my new diet. I don't crave approval for my decisions. In time he'll respect me for not eating the fattening foods. I *can* change!"

Lila changes her attitudes toward her third-grade class by realizing she makes herself angry, nobody else. She begins to learn *personal* management skills along with classroom management skills. She realizes her frustration and anger have to do with more than her job; but as she gains power over the decisions in her emotional life, she is better equipped to tackle the misbeliefs of anger and frustration. "It's okay not to be perfect," she tells herself. "I am not permanently lacking self-control. I *can* change and I *am* changing!"

When You Decide to Change

1. Write in your notebook the number of times each day you attribute your feelings to external events.
2. Write your negative verbal expressions in your notebook as soon as you can after you've said them.
3. Write a *better* way to handle things as we've outlined in this book.

Some notebook entries might look like this:

	MISBELIEF	TRUTH
8:00 a.m.	Felt lousy because of the rain.	I can be happy when it's raining if I choose to be.
10:30 a.m.	Said to Jimmy, "Your nagging makes me climb the walls!"	I make myself want to climb the walls when Jimmy nags.

	MISBELIEF	TRUTH
2:00 p.m.	Felt it's the committee's fault that I'm overworked. They let me do all the work.	I permit myself to be overworked. By suffering silently I invite more of the same.
10:00 p.m.	Was irritated at neighbors and felt like moving, although I didn't let them know about my feelings.	I allow myself to feel irritated and to suffer in silence. I can assert my feelings in a non-accusing way.

4. Make time in your day to correct the irrational thinking. Make it a definite time—lunch time, coffee break time, before bed, or whatever time is best for you. This is important. Knowing and recognizing irrational thinking is the first vital point. Secondly, knowing how to change those wrong thoughts is necessary. And lastly, *do* it—take action!

"The committee is not overworking me. I am allowing myself to be overworked. On Thursday at the meeting I am going to request some of my responsibilities be delegated to others."

"I allow myself to be upset at Jimmy's nagging. Nagging is learned behavior. I will start rewarding Jimmy for not nagging and for behaving in ways which are pleasing."

Admit to yourself that your negative thinking causes unhappiness. Take hold of the promise that the Lord gives to His people: I *will put a new spirit within you,* and allow your thinking to be dominated by the Holy Spirit. When you do this you will find that *consciously choosing* to change old falsehoods is more than a self-help notion; it's being strong in the Lord and in the power of His might.

You *can* change. The Bible is brimming with stories of changed lives through the power of God. Faith puts you in touch with the power of God. Nobody else can give you faith. You're the only one who can take the life of faith. You either take faith and believe in Jesus Christ and who you are in Him, or you wander along through life, a victim of circumstances, people, events, and situations you can't control.

Some people whose lives were radically changed by faith in God are Job (who insisted through his intense sufferings that God was still sovereign); Moses (who chose against being a ruler in the house of Egypt and joined the Jewish slaves to lead them out of slavery); Jacob (who waited and labored for a total of 14 years in order that he might marry Rachel); Joseph (who spent several years in prison for a crime he didn't commit); David (who spent years running from the wrath of King Saul); to name only a few. It would be safe to say that every man, woman and child who encounters and receives Jesus Christ as Savior and Lord of their lives experiences change. That change is conversion and regeneration of their souls as their spirits become alive, "which were born, not of blood, nor of the will of the flesh, nor of the will of man, but of God."[1]

> Therefore if any man be in Christ, he is a new creature; old things are passed away; behold, all things are become new.[2]

Changing Your Circumstances

Nothing in this chapter or this book implies that you should not attempt to change your circumstances where it's appropriate. We are not teaching simple quiescence and passivity in saying that where disparity between you and the circumstances exists, it is always and inflexibly the rule to work at changing yourself only.

At times you will want to alter your circumstances rather than to stay in them and concentrate on changing your self-talk. This includes asking other people to change behaviors that create problems for you.

When Jesus was preaching to the people of His divinity, He was almost stoned by the outraged Jews. "If I do not the works of my

1. John 1:13.
2. 2 Corinthians 5:17.

Father, believe me not," He told them. "But if I do, though ye believe not me, believe the works, that ye may know and believe that the Father is in me, and I in him." These words really infuriated them and they physically charged Him. Jesus got out of their way and escaped out of their hand. Then He went away beyond Jordan and lived at the place where John had baptized Him.[3]

He changed the circumstances.

At times you will want to alter your circumstances rather than to stay in them. You can change circumstances by asking other people to change behaviors that are especially troublesome, hurtful, or harmful. It is not true that you must remain in all painful situations and accept them as your lot in life. Often it is far more godly to change the situation than to bravely but needlessly continue to suffer.

You possess a precious and wonderful ability called choice.

God is not satisfied to let us continue living in the old fleshly ways that brought destruction, sickness, confusion, and suffering. He tells us, "A new heart also will I give you, and a new spirit will I put within you: and I will take away the stony heart out of your flesh, and I will give you an heart of flesh."[4]

And to the new person, the person who takes a stand against misbeliefs that deny the power and glory of God, He gives His blessing. "And he shall be like a tree planted by the rivers of water, that bringeth forth his fruit in his season; his leaf also shall not wither; and whatsoever he doeth shall prosper."[5]

"Repent ye therefore, and be converted [changed], that your sins may be blotted out, when the times of refreshing shall come from the presence of the Lord."[6]

If the cold-hearted Philippian jailer could change, so can you. If the woman of Samaria with her questionable reputation could

3. John 10:31–42.
4. Ezekiel 36:26.
5. Psalm 1:3.
6. Acts 3:19.

change and become an evangel of truth, you too can change. If the blood-thirsty Saul, persecutor of the Jews, could change and become the tender-hearted Saint Paul, loving writer of 13 books in the New Testament, you too can change.

Your attitudes, choices, and beliefs make you what you are.

10

Misbelief in Never Taking a Chance

When people believe they should never take a chance, they commonly misbelieve a number of related lies, such as:

1. One of life's most crucial objectives is to prevent getting hurt. No matter what, I shouldn't get hurt.

2. Taking chances could lead to calamity. I could get hurt if I take chances in life.

3. Being safe is of utmost importance. It is terrible to be in any kind of danger.

4. It's terrible to make a wrong decision.

5. If I take chances in life, I could lose vital things like money, friends, approval, time, security.

6. I should never lose anything. Losing something is terrible.

7. I don't dare make mistakes. Mistakes are terrible.

8. I must always think ahead and try to foresee every possible trouble and woe.

9. I must intricately plan all of my actions as well as the words I say in order to prevent loss, pain, and disgrace.

10. God doesn't approve of risk-taking behavior.

Roland arrives twenty minutes early for his first clinic appointment and, determined to make good use of his time, picks up a religious magazine in the waiting room. He has to force himself to read it, but such clenched-jaw determination is not unusual for him.

"I've been so tense and nervous lately I can hardly force myself to go to work," he explains as his interview begins. His smile is formed from the sheer obedience of lip muscles drawn back over bared teeth. There is nothing to smile about and no laughter shines in his eyes.

"It really doesn't bother me that much, but last month a guy who worked under me was promoted over me." He pauses, inhales, continues. "Ever since, I've been nervous about going to work." As the interview progresses it becomes apparent that Roland saw his job as he saw life: an obstacle course of temptations to risk-taking. His object: to get through the obstacles without taking risks or trying something new.

The man who got the promotion was someone who was willing to take what Roland regarded as totally unjustified chances with the company's capital and reputation. Suspecting what was going on behind his boss' closed door filled Roland with anxiety. In his opinion, the risks that were being taken were outrageous and dangerous.

Roland had never been responsible for a bad decision. He couldn't understand how other people who made risky decisions with the company's money and good name could get the major promotions while he sat in the background going nowhere. He thought his good reputation for doing what was best for the company should count for something.

At church he was on the board of deacons. The other board members often experienced friction at the meetings because of Roland's refusal to accept changes. When an effort was made to move the church in new directions or to change, Roland reacted in one of two ways: he vociferously objected or he retreated sullenly into silence.

Roland's wife presented additional anxieties. Just when they had paid off the mortgages on both their cars, she began to talk about buying a new home. To Roland this meant nothing more than a larger mortgage with no assurance they would ever have it paid off.

"I don't understand why other people don't recognize the soundness of my judgments," Roland complains.

Here's a man who rarely makes mistakes. He has nearly always played it safe and has bluntly refused to act if there were the slightest doubt about the consequences of his decisions. He was proud that he could look back on his life devoid of mistakes. He believed making positive choices was a skill.

Unfortunately, Roland didn't see that he actually made many mistakes and most of them serious ones. They weren't errors of judgment such as a person who behaves impulsively might make; they were quite different.

They were errors of omission.

"Roland, are you convinced that you would be seriously in the wrong if you were to take a chance in some situation?"

"I do believe that. And might I point out that because of my convictions I have a home almost paid off, a decent savings account, two paid-for cars . . ."

As he talks it becomes clear that his misbeliefs cause him intense anxiety. He defends his refusal to take risks, but doesn't understand why other people don't understand and appreciate his wisdom.

As a result of his misbeliefs, he has repeatedly avoided making decisions with an unpredictable outcome. He has chosen, instead, to do nothing or say nothing if the situation looks as if a risk may be involved. He takes the safest position possible on all points. Because of his safety seeking, he has failed to act responsibly on a number of occasions and failed to reap the rewards which people who are willing to take risks receive.

Roland's misbeliefs include:

1. God is definitely on the side of those who check and recheck to assure themselves of the safety of their choices.

2. It is unthinkable, even sinful, to make a decision which could eventuate in the loss of anything.

3. If a person makes a decision which turns out in retrospect to have been the wrong one, he then is stupid and guilty.

4. If a person makes a decision without absolute certainty of its outcome, it is sloppy and careless behavior.

5. God doesn't bless mistakes.

6. Protecting oneself and playing it safe, foreseeing and guarding against possible harm, is the aim and object of living.

In his attempts to avoid anxiety, Roland taught himself to be anxious. Avoiding anxiety meant contentment to Roland, but he never seemed to reach a place in his life where anxiety didn't exist.

Julia is a 57-year-old widow. Her doctor has advised her to move from the upper midwest of the United States to a warmer climate in the south, but the idea frightens her.

"I have roots here," she mumbles. "And I won't know anyone in a new town—everything will be so strange." Her eyes blink as she fights tears. She is very unhappy in her present home and her health is rapidly failing. If she doesn't get to a warmer, drier climate, she may die. But the idea of change is so threatening to her that she sees it as catastrophic. Suppose she makes a mistake? Suppose the town she moves to proves unfriendly and unwelcoming? Suppose she is lonely in the new place? Suppose, suppose, suppose? The anxiety is beyond endurance. She pulls a handkerchief from her sleeve and gives herself to sobs.

"Suppose you *do* make a mistake, Julia? What then?"

"What then? Why, there I'd be in a strange place, not knowing anyone. I'd be alone; oh, it would be dreadful!"

"Are you so very happy where you now live?"

"Oh, goodness, no! I'm very unhappy. My husband is gone, my children live in other parts of the country, I'm ill most of the time and I haven't much to do—"

But she still insists she couldn't make a move like the one the doctor advises. Too risky. She has taught herself not to take chances, even though she is now endangering her life by not following her doctor's orders.

Some people would actually rather die than change or take a chance. Paradoxically, the very thing they fear is what occurs by *not* taking the chance. It is not wisdom that causes a person to refuse risk. It is fear—fear of losing health, security, safety, familiarity, comfort, predictability, control, power. These are threats too great to risk.

Roland's feelings of frustration had increased to the point where he believed the whole world was falling apart. He felt threatened and unhappy at work after losing the promotion he felt he deserved, and he was frustrated and threatened at home by his wife's talking about buying a new home. The children offered new threats as they grew older and made decisions of their own, decisions Roland couldn't control or make conform to his fear-related demands. He was beleaguered and discomforted about so many things: the neighbors who bought a camper he knew they couldn't afford, the church's decision to buy property for a summer campground, the new tax laws, the weather, the price of gasoline, his son's desire to be a musician, his mother who refuses to go to a nursing home where she'd be safer but less happy than at home. He couldn't understand why people did the unreasonable things they did.

As Roland continued his therapy sessions, he began an inquisitive review of his habits. With help he was able to note situations where he had told himself paralyzing lies about taking risks.

It was painful for him to talk about his teen years. "I remember how unhappy I always felt—I was so lonely. If I wanted to call someone up or just hang around someone, I couldn't do it. If there was a group of kids standing together, I'd be afraid to walk over and join them. I was always afraid I'd be rejected, I guess. When I was younger, my mother used to make the calls for me. You know, like on Boy Scout night she'd call some other mother and make sure I had a ride, and she'd invite friends of hers over who had sons my age. She knew all the kids on the block and invited them over for special events she'd dream up—and somehow or another I got along all right. But when I got into my teens it seems as if everything just fell apart. I hated school even though everybody told me I was so smart. I wouldn't ask anyone to do anything with me. I wouldn't intentionally go up to someone and just start walking with them and talking, you know, the way the kids all did—"

"Do you know what made you behave this way?"

"Well, I think I was just terrified that they'd turn me down. You know, I'd call some kid up and ask him to come over to go somewhere and he'd say no. Good grief, I was so bound up and scared. Just thinking about it now makes me feel bad. Why is that?"

"Several reasons. For example, calling a friend would be taking a big chance, wouldn't it?"

"Yes. He might turn me down."

Roland's agitation mounted. He shredded his styrofoam coffee cup as he talked. "I knew I could do as well as the other kids in so many things, but I just didn't go out for them. Things like the debate team, sports—I just couldn't force myself to join in. It was so—so *lonely*. I was very angry, too. I had these fantasies about shooting people. Sometimes when I get frustrated and angry even now I find myself thinking about getting out a gun and standing in the middle of the lobby at work and firing."

Roland's misbeliefs had a strong hold over his thinking and his actions. Although chances are he would never actually act out his shooting fantasy, he was unhappy that he would think such thoughts. "I'm a Christian!" he cries. "How can such thoughts even enter my mind?"

When something is painful to us, we automatically want to get rid of it, whether that painful thing is a thought, action, event, situation or physical stimulus. "Mommy, make the ouchie go away!" the child cries. Mommy kisses the ouchie, strokes the child, coos,

142

prays and the child is assuaged. The adult feels pain and cries, "Help! Something! Somebody! Help!" When there is no answer and the pain still persists, he reaches into his bag of previously used coping devices. One of those devices to wipe out pain may be to wipe out the people who cause pain. It also may be to wipe out the presence of happy people who only remind him of his losses and pain. That's why we often feel relieved when we read about others who are suffering tragedy and loss or when we hear of someone else's failures. It somehow relieves us of our own personal anxieties. It says, "Hey, I'm not so bad off after all. Here's a guy whose house burned down and who lost his wife and four kids, and here's another guy who just went to jail for embezzling, and here's a movie star who's dead from an overdose of sleeping pills. What do you know, I'm all right after all."

Roland's desire to extinguish the pain he felt at being lonely and left out found expression in his shooting fantasies. He'd wipe out the pain by wiping out the people.

"I don't know why I was so afraid of being rejected. People were just so intimidating to me. Somebody once said if you don't try to make friends, you won't have any. Well, it's true. I stayed away by myself and nobody came out after me to try to make friends with me. I didn't look friendly. How could I? I was scared to death of everybody."

Roland's fear of risk robbed him of a happy and productive adolescence. His teen years were a muddle of sorrow and suffering because of his misbelief that it's terrible to take a risk.

He believed taking a risk could result in being rejected. Being rejected would be terrible. His misbeliefs were:

1. Nobody ought to reject me.
2. Everybody ought to be nice to me.
3. Nobody should hurt my feelings or not want to be with me.
4. It would be terrible if someone were to intentionally hurt my feelings.

LIES!

If you believe any of the above, please consider the truth for a moment.

God himself took the risk of great loss when He set out to build His kingdom. He took the greatest risk since the history of man when He sent His Son, Jesus, to the earth for our sakes. When Jesus began His ministry He risked the loss of His reputation, family, earthly security, home, popularity and friends—literally everything a person can lose—in order to do the will of His Father.

Look at the risk God took when He created man with a free will. He took the risk that man might use his will to rebel *against* God, his creator and protector. And that's just what happened.

As a result of God's risk, the very worst that could happen *did* happen. Man *did* rebel against Him and go his own way. "All we like sheep have gone astray,"[1] the Word of God tells us. "All have sinned, and come short of the glory of God."[2] Yet God created man perfect, blameless, sinless, holy and "good" in His sight; He created man in His own image![3] The risk He took was a big one and look what happened.

We can't conclude that God didn't know what He was doing or that because He took a risk He acted impulsively or without judgment (as we accuse ourselves of doing when we take risks). To God the stakes were so high that the risk was worth it.

God wants us to imitate Him. "Be ye therefore imitators of God" Ephesians 5:1 reads (NASB). As a follower of Christ, imitate Him. This includes imitating His willingness to take some risks. You can walk at times where you cannot see more than one step ahead and you can trust God for each step. You can trust God to work out consequences you cannot. You can believe risk-taking is healthy.

Faith itself is a risk. You must trust God and act in faith in order to take that step you cannot see. If you're going to walk on

1. Isaiah 53:6.
2. Romans 3:23.
3. Genesis 1:26.

water, you need to be willing to *take the chance* that you might sink to the bottom.

- You can't lead a happy, peaceful life without risks.
- To gain a friend, you have to take the risk of rejection.
- To have dates with the opposite sex, you risk being turned down or disliked.
- To speak up and be heard by others you risk rebuff, correction and censure.
- To be noticed, you risk being ignored.
- To get a job, you risk having your application turned down.
- To be a leader, you risk criticism and opposition.
- To gain a promotion at your work, you risk losing out to someone else.
- To win, you risk defeat.
- These risks are not bad.

The misbelief that it is stupid or sinful to make decisions which might turn out wrong is unfounded. We're told to be wise as serpents, harmless as doves.[4] Wisdom does not mean acting in fear or cowardice.

Perfect love casts out fear[5] means to us that the love of God has wiped out the power of fear over our lives if we will use God's methods of conquering it. "Cast your fears [cares] on Me!"[6] He explains. "Give them to Me! I know what to do with them." It is in this way we are set free to take risks.

Then whether we succeed or fail is not our utmost concern. We are not enslaved by fear of negative results. We willingly allow ourselves possible failure, possible negative results. Painful fear and anxiety no longer play a dominant role in our lives.

4. Matthew 10:16.
5. 1 John 4:18.
6. 1 Peter 5:7 (paraphrased).

The Christian walking by the Spirit, in the will of God, can trust that outcomes of his actions in faith are totally in the hands of the Father. The truth for the Christian is that disaster, catastrophe, or utter defeat *cannot occur.* We have no business thinking in those terms!

God never fails.

An adage that rings true for the child of God is "Nothing ventured, nothing gained." Moses, leading Israel into the desert; Abraham, leaving his home with no idea of his final destination; Daniel, continuing to pray contrary to the law of the king; the apostles who preached Jesus crucified, risen and coming again in spite of horrendous reprisals—were all *taking risks.* They ventured with the certain knowledge that if they did not venture, they could not gain.

> I count all things but loss for the excellency of the knowledge of Christ Jesus my Lord: for whom I have suffered the loss of all things, and do count them but dung, that I may win Christ.[7]

These words are not the words of an unfulfilled man driven with anxiety that he might lose something precious. Saint Paul here was willing to risk everything there was to risk because he knew with absolute certainty whom he belonged to, and a relationship with Jesus Christ was more important to him than his own comfort and life.

Everyone at some point or another in his life makes decisions without the benefit of knowing the consequences. Our unhappy friend, Roland, began to realize this fact, and once he did, he started identifying his own misbeliefs about taking chances. Using our three-point system, he *identified, argued,* and *replaced* his misbeliefs with the truth, in that order. It was not a quick process by any means.

Misbelief:

It's sinful to make a mistake.

7. Philippians 3:8.

Argument:

Mistakes are not necessarily sinful. Many mistakes result from the fact that as a human being I am not omniscient, and there is nothing wicked about that. If I make a mistake due to acting in the flesh, I have a Savior to save me from my own mistakes and to lead me in the ways of truth. I don't want to walk in the flesh and I don't want to make mistakes due to ignorance, but to the best of my knowledge, I'm doing neither, so I now choose to act in faith, even though I know I am taking the risk of making a mistake.

Replaced with Truth:

I have put too much value on being right and being accepted at all times. It is not vital for me to be accepted and 100% right at all times. God does not fail. My faith and trust is in Him. In the past I have tried to be my own lord, but now by taking risks I give Him lordship over my life.

Roland realized it wouldn't be the end of the world if he invited a friend to go bowling or fishing and he was rejected. He realized it wasn't the end of the world if he didn't always take the safest, most sure way. "I know I don't have to play it safer than Jesus does," he reasoned. He discovered he could stand it even if he was rejected, even if his decisions didn't turn out as he wanted or expected! He could stand it!

Learning to take acceptable risks with his career and finances was more difficult for Roland to do because the stakes were higher, but he made progress here, too, by doggedly opposing misbeliefs with the truth. He then acted upon what he knew to be true.

You can help yourself to change, too. If you have harbored any of the misbeliefs about risk-taking which we have discussed in this chapter, you can work to change those beliefs and your behavior.

Check the behaviors below which you *avoid* because they seem to you to be too risky:

____ Telling someone else your true weak points, sins or mistakes.

____ Investing money in something which stands a good chance of paying off handsomely.

____ Asking for a date.

____ Accepting a date.

____ Asking for a raise.

____ Telling someone you like him/her very much.

____ Telling someone you love him/her.

____ Talking up to someone who has in the past intimidated you.

____ Telling someone your wants or needs.

____ Inviting someone to accept Jesus as Savior and Lord.

____ Talking to a stranger in a waiting room or on a bus.

____ Asking someone (not in your family) to spend an evening/ afternoon/morning with you.

This is not an all-inclusive list, so please ask the Lord to call to your mind areas in which you are afraid of risk-taking. Name especially those areas where God-pleasing action is required. The Holy Spirit will quicken these to your mind. Now write them out in your notebook. Write the misbeliefs about risk-taking which prevent your acting appropriately in each situation.

Here is an example from one person's notebook:

"*Misbelief:* It's wrong to let someone know about my weak points. I am afraid of taking the risk that's involved in telling someone else about my weak points. The misbelief I keep repeating to myself is that such self-revelations are terribly personal and dangerous to reveal. If I open up to someone, he/she might turn on me and reject me one day. Then I'll wish I had never shared such deep and personal things about myself. Besides, what if he/she thinks less of me when I reveal my true feelings? That would be dreadful. I'd feel all broken up. It's just safer not to tell too much about yourself. It's safer to keep your distance."

After you have written in your notebook, compare your misbelief with the following scriptures and ask yourself these questions:

1. "But what things were gain to me, those I counted loss for Christ."[8] *Am I willing to accept loss for Jesus' sake?*

2. "Without faith it is impossible to please him: for he that cometh to God must believe that he is, and that he is a rewarder of them that diligently seek him."[9] *Am I willing to act in faith by believing in Him with my whole being?*

3. Read the parable of the talents in Matthew 25:14–30 where the Lord teaches us that He expects us to take risks. If we do not take risks, we cannot effectively put to work the precious gifts the Lord has given to us. If we don't take risks, we won't use any of the gifts of the Spirit, we won't witness for Jesus, we won't pray for anyone's healing, won't invite someone else to pray for us, won't generously give to the house of God, won't love, forgive, worship or ask in order that it be given us. We won't move ahead in the areas the Lord calls us to. Instead, we will bury everything God has given us in the cold relentless ground just as the servant did in this parable. God clearly objects to fear of risk-taking by this parable.

Listen to the Words You Tell Yourself

Sometimes the words you tell yourself never form to make clear, concise sentences. They are more like impressions. Julia, the woman who refuses to move to a warmer climate for her health's sake, didn't realize what she was telling herself at first because she never actually said to herself, "I am now going to tell myself the misbelief

8. Philippians 3:7.
9. Hebrews 11:6.

that it would be terrible to be alone and in a strange town." It was more of an anxious feeling she experienced as she pictured herself stranded and lonely in a strange place.

But once you *identify* your misbeliefs, *argue* against them. "No, it would *not* be terrible to be alone and in a strange town. God has promised me quite clearly and vividly that He would never leave nor forsake me! It's silly of me to doubt that. Besides, there are churches and wonderful Christians in every town in the country. It will be exciting to meet and make new Christian friends. It will be an adventure. I thank God that He has provided me with adventure and excitement at this stage of my life!"

Never miss an opportunity to replace a misbelief with the truth.

If you will put effort into changing, you will develop habits that will last throughout your life. Each time a misbelief enters your thought-life, you'll recognize it as such and argue against it, replacing it with the truth. JESUS CHRIST IS LORD OVER MY LIFE!

The Change

In order to work best, this technique for extinguishing your fearful behavior should at first be taken in small steps. Start out by attacking the little risks that aren't paralyzing, then progress step-by-step to larger risks. The effect of such progressive risk-taking will be:

1. To teach you to *seek the Lord* for His will in situations in which you have felt fear.
2. To *trust the Lord* to act on your behalf according to His will.
3. To *obey the Lord* by following His directions for action.
4. To experience the *blessing of the Lord* by working through your anxieties with Him.

By actually doing the thing you fear, you overcome the fear of it. Make sense? It will as you gradually progress from one risk to another. If you haven't listed anything but major risks in your notebook, go back and seek the Lord to show you some smaller ones you can start to work on. From there, progress through the others, and watch the change occur in your life. You may feel, as Roland did after he signed the papers on his new house, "I'm experiencing something entirely new in my life—peace!"

Misbelief in Our Relationships with Others

The distraught woman's voice is high-pitched and loud. She speaks with short breaths, snapping the ends of her sentences as though she were chewing them off with her teeth.

"That husband of mine doesn't do a thing around this house! The place could fall apart for all he cares! *I'm* the one who shovels the walk, mows the lawn, fixes the broken light switch, takes out the garbage—what does he do? Nothing!"

According to this woman, her husband obviously is not fulfilling his end of the marriage bargain. She continues, "When the car dies, who calls the service station? *I* do. When the hot water heater broke last fall, who saw to it that it was fixed? *I* did. I do everything around our house. You name it."

So far in her collection of diatribes she is unjustified. Where is it written in the law that the man does the mowing, shoveling, and fixing?

"But I also do the cooking, the cleaning, the chauffeuring, the disciplining of the kids, the shopping. You name it. My husband should do the man's work."

This beleaguered woman firmly believes her husband is not fulfilling his obligations as the man of the house. "A man is supposed to do the fixing and the muscle work!"

In other words, her husband is supposed to *meet her expectations*. He falls short of her expectations and offends her personal Law of the Man's Obligations; therefore, he is in the wrong, a cad and not a man—in her opinion, that is.

Wives are not the only ones with a list of expectations they insist be met. Take the husband who is horrified at the idea that his wife wants to go to work and hire a housekeeper to do his laundry and clean the house. "A woman's place is in the home!" he protests. He can't figure out how she could insult his expectations like this.

"I don't wash dishes," he stoutly maintains. "That's women's work." He's alarmed that his wife is interested not only in going to work, but there's the chance she might earn the same salary or more than he. His Law of the Woman's Obligations says she's in the wrong, unfair, not a woman.

Putting others under the law—under my own expectations—means telling myself that others owe it to me to live up to my expectations, whether I'm wrong or right. This is one of the best methods around for making yourself miserable. You'll make others miserable, too, and not even realize why.

When you dream up a list of obligations for others, you're leaving yourself wide open for disappointment. These arbitrary obligations you put others under are not in accord with the Word of God at all.

Nowhere in the Word of God does it say to the husband, "Thou shalt shovel the walk, mow the lawn and do all the repairs on the house," and nowhere in the Word does it say, "Woman, thou shalt not leave the house, nor shalt thou ever require thy husband to do the dishes."

Your life can be a nightmare network of obligations—not only the Law of Obligations you put on others, but also the obligations others place upon you.

Carrie is a woman who is always busy, one of those people who is always out of breath when she answers the telephone. You feel you're taking her time by requiring she say hello when you call her. She works harder than anyone you know, but if you ask her for a favor, she'll always comply.

She finally confessed wearily one day, "I'm pressured, overworked, always running around for other people. I feel like a windup toy. Just push the button and I'll do something nice."

Carrie did most of her activities out of a false sense of obligation. She cleaned her house out of obligation (I'm *supposed* to have a clean house!); she cared for her children with far more fuss than they really needed out of obligation (After all, my husband's mother sewed all her kids' clothes; I ought to, too!); she ran errands for others, helped her own parents in every way she could, served on various committees for school and church, entertained at least twice a week, served as a volunteer for the local hospital and, in addition, she resolutely and laboriously served only homemade pasta, baked only homemade breads *and* twice a week she ironed sheets and pillow cases. If she had the time, she'd do a neighbor's laundry and ironing as well.

She was a slave to obligation. Most of her busy-ness she did not choose out of desire to serve but out of a false standard of requirements.

Carrie's social life was a response to her lists of "oughts." "We *ought* to have the Ricci's over; they had us over last week." Or, "Valarie sent me a birthday card; I ought to send her one." Or, "Jimmy gave my little Artie an expensive gift at the Christmas exchange. We ought to give him an expensive gift, too."

She went out of her way to do something for others because she felt she *ought* to. She invited people to her home because she felt she *ought* to. She accepted invitations because she felt she *ought* to. She offered expressions of sympathy, congratulations, farewells and greetings because she owed them.

Carrie is only one of the never-ending stream of people whose lives are in a snarl because of the misbelief that human relationships are alliances of obligation.

There are only two basic obligations, two things we *ought* to do: "Love the Lord thy God with all thy heart, and with all thy soul, and with all thy mind . . . love thy neighbor as thyself."[1]

God is concerned with *quality* in our relationships. Quality is obtained only through love. Love says, "It's all right with me if you be you. It's all right with me if I be me, too. That means I set you free from the obligations and expectations I might contrive. I set myself free from your unrealistic obligations and expectations, too."

God is deeply interested in your relationships with others and wants to be placed in the center of them so that He becomes the focal point of your affections and cares. His heart is motivated by love.

FALSE OBLIGATION SAYS:	THE OBLIGATION OF LOVE SAYS:
"I must because I owe it."	"I will because I choose to."
"I should because it's expected of me."	"I want to because I care."
"I ought to because I'm supposed to."	"I'd like to."

It's a matter of bondage versus liberty; law versus freedom; letter and code versus Spirit and life.

For some Christians the words *I choose* are part of a strange, unheard-of vocabulary! They are so enslaved to legalistic demands that the only time they feel relief from guilt is when they are saying, "I *must*." Carrie confessed that she felt the most holy when she was pressured and overworked, pursuing a battalion of "musts."

1. Matthew 22:37–39.

The words I *ought to* are preludes to feelings of guilt. Carrie tells herself, "I *ought* to have my mother to dinner," and then, because she doesn't really *want* to, pleading lack of time or a conflicting schedule, she doesn't have her mother to dinner. She feels guilty. "I *should have had* my mother to dinner."

If she really had wanted to have her mother to dinner, she would have done it. If she had *chosen* to, it is more than likely she would have altered her schedule. Or, as an alternative, Carrie could call her mother and invite her for next week, giving her an invitation to look forward to and giving herself good feelings about her choice.

Suppose God created us as automatons, rigidly programmed to do His will. Suppose we were wired so that we couldn't possibly do anything contrary to His commands. Would He then have people who acted in *love?* Can a machine doing its function be said to *love?*

God's love is a love of *free choice*. What wonderful words those are! True freedom is the opportunity to *choose* to act and live as you ought. We have the glorious opportunity to discover the personality of Jesus, to choose love over manipulation, guilt, and false obligation.

How happy is the marriage where the husband and wife eke out an existence amid each other's expectations? ("You're *supposed* to carry in the groceries. My father always carried in the groceries," or "You're *supposed* to fold my socks in little mounds. My mother always did.") You're supposed to—you're obligated to me!

The answer is not to learn to love everything we do for one another; it's learning to stop hurling unloving and ungodly demands at each other. If we were allowed the right to choose our acts in love, to live according to the Gospel of Christ rather than the Gospel of Each Other, we would make some amazing discoveries about ourselves and our relationships.

Your expectations hurt yourself as well as others. When you demand that others fulfill your expectations, you make yourself a target for defeat. What happens to *you* when others don't do as you want them to? What happens to *you* when others don't help you, care for you, treat you the way you think they ought to? What happens when someone says or does something to blight your expectations of him or her? Suppose someone close to you doesn't measure up to your expectations in the areas of achievement, success, education, skills, or personal happiness? What happens when these expectations you've taught yourself to have are sitting out on your window ledge, flopping in the wind—fruitless, empty, bringing no returns?

Below are non-biblical, non-spiritual demands and expectations and their results when unmet.

EXPECTATIONS	RESULTS IF NOT MET
Husbands' and wives' demands of each other.	Feeling hurt, unloved, rejected, angry, unfulfilled, depressed.
Friends' demands of each other.	Feeling hostile, unappreciated, disapproved of, unsuccessful, rejected, unworthy.
Children's demands of parents; parents' demands of children.	Feeling unloved, unwanted, unworthy, failure, anger, lost identity.

Picture yourself as free from obligations to others based on false premises. Picture yourself free to act in love and out of choice. You are free *from:*

1. What other people might think or say about you.
2. What other people expect you to be and do.
3. The expectations you try to bind others with which only leave you frustrated and miserable because others rarely live up to your demands.

You are free *to:*

1. Choose to be and do all that God has planned for you.
2. Love your neighbor (husband, wife, children, friends) as yourself.

Visualize yourself being moved by the Holy Spirit from within, in much the same manner as a tree is motivated to sprout leaves or bear fruit. It's natural! You *are* a loving person, made so by the new creation of Jesus and by the indwelling of His own Spirit. Look at yourself as God does. You're a person given a choice to love other people and love yourself without fear, manipulation, guilt, or obligation.

The Bible tells us that it is *love* that fulfills the law,[2] not duty or responsibility or obligation. "For he who loves his neighbor has fulfilled the law."[3]

Is "I Want To" Bad?

Some Christians have a deep suspicion of their own desires. They avoid saying, "I want to," and are more likely to say something like, "I think I *should* . . ." or "I feel impressed to . . ." or "I feel led to . . ." These righteous-sounding phrases are all fine and good, but will fit together with the glory of choice only if we admit that we *want*. Which of the following would you prefer were said to you?

"I feel I *should* come over to visit you,"

or

"I *want* to come over to visit you."

How about sentences like:

"I feel impressed to ask you to dinner."

"I really would be so happy if you'd have dinner with me. I want you to. Will you?"

"I feel led to marry you."

"I love you and want you to marry me."

There is nothing wicked about your desires when they are in line with the Word of God. The Word of God says that God *gives* you the desires of your heart.

2. Romans 13:10.
3. Romans 13:8 (RSV).

> Delight thyself also in the LORD; and he shall give thee the desires
> of thine heart.[4]

Notice it says first to delight yourself in the Lord. When your
delight is in Him and His ways, your desires become His desires.
They are pure and honoring to Him. The lusts of the flesh are evil
because they aren't God's ways. Selfish and ungodly wants and
desires need to be laid at the foot of the cross.

You're a new person when you are a Christian. When the Holy
Spirit of God within you guides and motivates you, you are a
completely different person from the self-seeking sinner you once
were.

> If any man be in Christ, he is a new creature: old things are passed
> away; behold, all things are become new.[5]

The question is, do you really believe you're a completely new
person? "According to your faith be it unto you."[6] Are you still
prowling around in your old sins and false expectations and problems? Or are you being set free from them?

Here is the marvelous possibility for every Christian:

> I have been crucified with Christ; it is no longer I who live, but
> Christ who lives in me.[7]

This new person is so identified with Jesus living within you
that you have the same desires He does. And since the desires of
Jesus are pure and loving, the desires of your new self can also be
pure and loving.

If you do occasionally miss the mark and give in to the desires
of the flesh or the suggestions of Satan, confess it immediately to
God and receive His forgiveness and cleansing. That's why we need

4. Psalm 37:4.
5. 2 Corinthians 5:17.
6. Matthew 9:29.
7. Galatians 2:20 (RSV).

to "test everything."[8] The fellowship of other Christians will help us to test and discern when we are uncertain about choices. They can sound an alarm when we are wrong. The Scriptures and our own consciences will serve as warning systems, too, helping us in the task of testing our desires.

Manipulation by Guilt

How do you make your desires known to those around you? When you don't identify your desires and tell people about them clearly, you run the risk of making people feel guilty in order to get your own way. Instead of honestly and clearly making your desires known, you manipulate people by making them feel guilty to get what you want. Manipulation is a hurtful behavior and guilt is a hurtful feeling. Did you ever hear anyone say how terrific guilt feels? Probably not.

Speaking the truth is a skill you can learn, remembering to keep accusations, threats, and hostility out. Here are some examples of manipulation by guilt and speaking the truth. Which would you rather someone spoke to you?

MANIPULATION BY GUILT	SPEAKING HONESTLY
I'm so exhausted, worn out, pooped from working all day and then overtime, too. I don't mind all the overtime (a lie) because I know how you have your heart set on buying that new car. I'm glad to work the overtime (a lie) so we can buy it for you. I'm really tired, though (truth). Working so hard really gets to me. I just don't know where I'll get the energy to drive Billy to his Scout meeting tonight.	I'm tired tonight. Would you please drive Billy to his Scout meeting tonight?

Love doesn't manipulate. Love dares to tell the truth.

8. 1 Thessalonians 5:21.

Sometimes a person will be so accustomed to manipulating by making people guilty, they can't recognize *love* when they see it!

MANIPULATION SAYS:	LOVE SAYS:
Nobody ever calls me. The phone hardly ever rings. Of course, I always call you. In fact, I called you twice last week.	You are under no obligation to me whatsoever. I love you without strings attached.
Did you know Shirley's husband brings her flowers every Friday? He must really love her. Of course, nobody ever brings me flowers.	Darling, it would make me so happy if you would buy me some flowers. I want you to bring me flowers. Will you?
I haven't got a ride to church. I walk 12 blocks in the snow and cold, but that's all right. I don't mind.	Would you mind stopping by and giving me a ride to church? No? That's all right. I do not hold you responsible for my comforts.

You stop manipulating when you come right out and state what it is you want. Manipulation plays on guilt. If you can make someone feel guilty, you can get them to do what you want. It's hardly the way of the Lord.

Mr. and Mrs. L. were tormented over their 16-year-old daughter's behavior. She was out every night, drinking and smoking, riding around with her gang and being intimate with boys. Her parents felt they had failed her terribly. They had raised their daughter with the idea that they owed her something for bringing her into the world. Mrs. L. was pregnant before her wedding to Mr. L. and they both felt guilty about that. They tried to give their daughter everything they could to make life worthwhile for her and, in a way, it was atoning. They sacrificed and scrimped on their small salaries and sent her to the best private schools, bought her expensive clothing, gave her private lessons in piano, ballet, violin, horseback riding, skiing and figure skating. They plied her with toys, games, beautiful furnishings, gave her parties, outings, summers at camp, whatever it was she wanted or expressed a desire for. They loved their girl dearly, but it was tainted with obligation and guilt.

By the time they sought Christian counseling, Mrs. L. had taught herself a raft of unsuccessful manipulative behaviors. She was confused and frustrated because her daughter wasn't submitting to her demands and laws of obligation. Mr. L., too, was at a loss for answers; in spite of his threats, admonitions, outbursts, tears, demands, and guilt-inducing accusations about how much he and Mrs. L. had done for her, nothing worked. Their daughter was out doing her own thing in direct defiance of their wishes.

Mr. and Mrs. L. had to learn how to release their lists of expectations and deposit them at the foot of the cross. Instead of using manipulation-by-guilt techniques, they needed to learn to speak truthfully and lovingly.

MANIPULATIVE	TRUTHFULLY
Suzie, you're rarely home lately and we sit here alone worrying about you night after night.	We want you to stay home tonight and be with us. We'll play some games and make a nice night of it.
What do you mean you don't want to be with us, your own parents? Do you realize all we've sacrificed for you and now you don't want to spend one little old evening with us—the two people on this earth who truly love you?	We can understand that you'd like to go out with your friends tonight, but you'll have to call it off. We want to be together as a family and have an evening together.
To think of the years of doing for you, going without, giving you everything we could to make life happy for you!	You're special. That's why we love you.

The conversation with Suzie did not end there. It took time for her to adjust to nonmanipulative behavior as well as to make some changes in her own attitudes and actions.

The Lord Jesus stands ready to lead us into all truth by the power of the Holy Spirit. He has set us free from the law of sin and death. The old law of demands, obligations, and expectations shall no more rule over us. We are now under the law of grace. We're free.

Carrie sought professional help for her problems because she thought she was losing control of her life. Her relationships were in a discouraging tangle of obligations. She told herself she owed everybody, and she rarely did anything without first convincing herself that she *must* do it. Her deep resentments and unremitting feelings of guilt had added up to a diagnosis of depressive neuroses.

She had to be shown that Jesus' perfect work of atonement had literally broken those chains of legalism in her relationships. She needed to see she didn't need chains like these to make her a good person. Her personhood depended upon what Jesus did on the cross, not what other people thought of her.

A new and loving freedom finally did replace the self-invented obligations in her relationships. She wrote a letter to her therapist some months after her therapy concluded. We'd like to share it with you:

> . . . *I can actually experience the love of Jesus flowing through me to other people for the first time in my life. I am now getting up in the morning and living through each day, not because I must in order to repay or satisfy someone's demands, but because I want to serve. . . . It's wonderful. I think the happiest day in my life was the day I threw out the word* obligation *from my thinking. . . . Thanks!*

Your relationships deserve your truthfulness and love. You deserve the respect and happiness such relationships bring.

12

Misbelief in Being Indispensable

"I'm sorry to be telephoning you at this hour," the cheerless voice begins. You reach for the lamp by the bed. It's three in the morning. "I—uh, that's uh, all right," you mutter somewhat unintelligibly.

"You're just the only person I could turn to," the voice continues. "I suppose I woke your wife up, too, like the last time I called. I'm really sorry."

"Uh, that's all right." You look over at your wife, who is sitting upright in bed and frowning unpleasantly at the clock. The ringing of the telephone woke the baby, whose wails now fill the air. Your wife gets to her feet mumbling something about justice.

"Yes, uh, sure," you say with a slight groan. "It's—it's, uh, all right if you come over now."

Getting phone calls like this after midnight is nothing new. People invade you at all hours of the day and night if they choose to. You have been proud to say that your life is a veritable open door for those in need.

From time to time the sneaking villains of reality poke up to startle you, but you shrug them off with righteous-sounding words like, "I've got to be willing to sacrifice in order to minister to the needs of others." You tell yourself you're learning to be "dead to self," but is that what it's really called when you're blind with fatigue and your own family suffers because of it?

Consider the experience of a young minister named John. He and his wife, Jan, had an exciting coffee house ministry with over 500 young people a week going through their doors. The energetic couple was well known and respected among the area churches and received financial support from them. Everything looked great from all standpoints.

Several of the young people helped out in the physical labors of the ministry, but the entire burden of spiritual leadership was on John and Jan's shoulders. They did all the counseling, preaching and teaching, in addition to overseeing every other aspect of the ministry. John and Jan worked day and night for a period of three years with no vacation time off and very little time to be alone together. Their recreation and relaxation always centered around and included the young people. Night after night both John and Jan burned the late hour candles counseling some young person in need.

The ministry flourished. Hundreds of young people came to know the Lord as Savior and many were helped out of deep troubles, including drug addiction, vagrancy, sexual problems, and criminal offenses.

But then suddenly and for no apparent reason, Jan became ill. She was confined to her bed unable to move her legs. In a month she was up and around, only to have a relapse in a few weeks and return to her bed. She recovered again, but in a short time was back in bed with the same symptoms. She and her husband attributed her condition to an attack of the devil who wanted to destroy their ministry.

They didn't see the weapons he was using.

They had given every breathing moment to their ministry while their marriage slowly and insidiously crumbled. No time for each other, for rest or relaxation, their personal strength all but vanished. Weariness, worry, illness, overwork, strain; then harsh words, arguments, cold silences, prayerlessness crept in—they were in big trouble long before it showed.

Their problems notwithstanding, the ministry continued on. John and Jan couldn't see what was happening. Looking back over the events that led up to the disastrous finale, they reasoned that their troubles all began at the time of Jan's first illness.

"We prayed and prayed for Jan's healing!" they said. "We *believed* God would answer our prayers! But He didn't answer the way we wanted Him to."

John asked the same question over and over. "Why did the Lord allow her to get sick?"

If you'll look carefully at this situation, you'll see it's not surprising that Jan became ill. How else could she legitimately take a rest? A holiday or a vacation was out of the question. The only way her body could find relief would be to go to bed sick. Because of a weakened physical condition, overworked nerves and tired reflexes, she was just ripe for a debilitating illness like the one she got.

The only means to assure not being overworked, pressured, run-down and faced with a disintegrating marriage was to stay ill. She didn't realize what was happening, however. She didn't intentionally get sick. Her spiritual tuning fork wasn't in use—she was given to the flesh.

The Lord gives us an example of the overworked man of God in the experience of Moses in Exodus 18:1–26. Jethro, Moses' father-in-law, saw how worn out Moses was as a counselor and judge. From morning to night the poor man was listening to the complaints and troubles of the children of Israel. He was just plain worn out. Jethro wisely saw that one man cannot do the work of the Lord *alone*. Moses was a mighty man of God and one of God's greatest servants, but he was not Mr. Indispensable.

"What is this thing that you are doing for the people?" Jethro asked. "Why do you *alone* sit as judge and all the people stand about you from morning to evening?"

Now Moses was a man with a sense of duty, a man well acquainted with the pressures and demands of his calling, not one to shirk his responsibilities, no. "Because the people come to me to inquire of God," he answered simply.

That's what John and Jan thought, too. The need is great! Look at all the troubles! We must do all we can to help! We are the only ones who can do it!

Jethro was firm and wise in his reply to Moses. "*The thing you are doing is not good,*" he told him.

He continued: "*You will surely wear out, both yourself and these people who are with you, for the task is too heavy for you; you cannot do it alone*" (verse 18).

Notice he told him that not only would Moses wear out, but *his people* as well!

John and Jan lost their coffee house ministry, not because of Jan's illness, but because they thought they were indispensable, the *only ones* to carry the full burden for the work God had given them. Pride, ambition, desire to succeed, fear of failure, and spiritual dishonesty were rampant. They lost their spiritual eyesight and energy first and then they lost the ministry.

The devil is very clever. He will tempt the Christian worker with something that has every appearance of good. What could be more noble than the desire to help people? What could be more Christian than working night and day for the Lord? Let's look for some of the subtle signs of the crossbones that could contaminate the pure in heart.

When Good Isn't So Good

The born-again Christian worker is not easily tempted in areas of overt, blatant sin (robbing banks, peddling drugs, becoming hit-men for the Mafia), so the devil gets us on our own turf by appealing to our *flesh* while convincing us it's the Spirit. He can skillfully and cunningly use pride, envy, greed, jealousy, anger, lust, gluttony, sloth (the Seven Deadly Sins!) as *motives* for our do-gooding and people-helping.

Howzzat? you say.

Let's elucidate.

- The man with feelings of inferiority gets saved and then takes on an attitude of superiority over the non-Christians of the world. He preaches on street corners and pigeon-holes everyone he can with the information that they are going straight to hell if they don't shape up. (Pride.)

- The minister who knows all the answers. Has all the solutions. Has all the revelation. He does not train any counselors in the church. He tells his people to come only to him with their troubles, nobody else. (Pride.)

- The prayer-group leader who spends more time eating and finding fault with others than praying. (Gluttony. Greed. Anger.)

- The Bible study leader who seethes inside every time one of the more talkative members of the group takes up too much time telling her/his points-of-view. (Anger. Envy. Pride.)

- The Christian worker who bad-mouths another worker's ministry because it's more successful. (Jealousy.)

- The church elder who is easily flattered by the attention of attractive women. (Pride. Lust.)

- The church worker who throws temper tantrums at home and tells himself the world is against him. (Anger.)

- The Christian worker who is always late, undependable, over-worked, tired, nervous, worried, and demanding of others. (Sloth.)

The desire to help people is a good one. The desire to serve the Lord by preaching, teaching, and counseling is certainly good. God wants us to serve Him by helping people, yet we can thwart His glorious will by a lack of spiritual wisdom and understanding—and something else, which we will talk about next.

The Greatest Good

It's possible to be a preacher, a teacher, a leader and even a martyr without giving the slightest hoot about people. You could pastor a church, lead Bible studies, travel the world preaching, or be persecuted for your faith in God without knowing anything at all about love. That's what 1 Corinthians 13 says. It says we can preach, and teach, move mountains with our faith, give all we own to the poor people, get ourselves martyred at the stake and it's all to no avail without love.

"You're the only person I can turn to," the troubled person tells you. "There's nobody else. You're the only one who can help me." You're in the position of being savior. You swallow it up; after all, you *do* love to help. You're the one with the answers and solutions, the big shot. You're like Moses.

Listen to these misbeliefs:

1. I am the Called One and the anointing to help and direct others is upon me alone.
2. I've got something special and unique from the Lord that nobody else has. It's up to me to deliver my revelation to the world.
3. Nobody else can do the job I do as well as I.
4. No matter what time of day or night it may be, I must always make myself available to meet all the needs of all others.
5. Jesus expects me to give up all my rights to privacy, rest and recreation if I am to serve Him fully.
6. In order to serve God with my whole heart, I must put my family second to my ministry.
7. I've given my children to the Lord so that the Holy Spirit can teach and guide them because I have no time to do this in my life as a Christian worker.

8. God has called me to help certain people and if it weren't for me, they would be in pitiful shape.

9. It's my Christian duty to provide all the answers and solutions to the people God has called me to help. If I don't, the consequences are on my head.

10. Others should recognize my calling and be of help and support to me in the work God has called me to.

11. If someone is less spiritual than I, he has no right being in the ministry; furthermore, he has no right to be more successful than I!

Are you believing any of these lies?

Your spiritual warning flag should fly high each time you hear yourself say anything at all related to "I'm indispensable." Pastor X told us how he nearly ruined his life and ministry in the early years of his work in the pastorate. "I prayed to the Lord about the number of people who came to my office daily for counseling. I could see that the needs were great, and I felt a little fearful because these people were expecting me to give them answers. I wasn't really that sure of myself. I prayed like this: 'Lord, I am going to trust you to bring me only the right number of people so I don't overwork myself. And bring me the ones I *can* help, not the ones I can't.'"

He cleared his throat and continued. "Everything went smoothly at first, and I actually had time for eight hours of sleep at night and some free time for my family, too. But then—pow! It hit. You see, I didn't allow anyone else to counsel because I didn't think anyone else was qualified. After all, *I* was the pastor. I didn't allow anyone else to preach or teach, and I oversaw all the church government decisions as well. I was overrun with work. I tried to answer everyone's problems and troubles—I wanted to be everything to everyone. I rarely had a day for my own family and I was wearing thin."

John and Jan would have benefited from the older pastor's experience. "It was about the time when I was on the verge of a nervous breakdown that the Lord showed me I was wrong. For one thing, I was binding myself to a prayer that no longer applied. I had *told* the Lord what to do and then I wondered how come what I told Him to do wasn't working out anymore. Well, it simply didn't apply anymore. So I made some changes, thank God! I delegated responsibilities to other people. I was shocked to discover how spiritual and capable my people were. I no longer did all the counseling alone. In fact, I don't think I'm as good a counselor as some of the others on my staff. I probably never was. I *thought* I was indispensable. I thought I was the only one who could help the people."

There is a time to change your unhappy situation and not remain in it. Sadly, and too often, the changes don't come soon enough. You are the only one who can make the changes. Waiting for the situation to change is not the answer.

The Truth

Pastor X took a step back before it was too late. He relinquished his grandiose ideas of himself. He told himself the *truth*. Compare the following with the list of misbeliefs on pages 154 and 155.

The truth:

1. I am *not* the only called-of-God person to help and direct others.
2. I am indeed special and unique, but so are other ministers of God. My ministry is not the most important one on earth.
3. Other people can minister equally as well as I.
4. Jesus always took time out from ministering to relax and refresh himself (Matt. 14:23) and so must I.
5. Jesus does not expect me to behave compulsively and impulsively. He expects me to serve Him with wisdom and a peaceful heart. A peaceful heart is one that finds rest in the midst of a storm.

6. In order to serve God with my whole heart, I must care for my family as He has called me to. If I neglect the precious souls He has given to me as my own kin, I neglect my first calling.

7. My children are my responsibility and I will not neglect them. God has given them to me and I will make sure I have time for them every day.

8. God has called me to help people, but God could help them without me. I rejoice that He sees fit to use me while realizing people would not be in pitiful shape without me.

9. It is an honor to be used of God. I realize, however, that I am not responsible for providing the answers and solutions to everyone's problems. He is the Savior—I am His servant. I can point to the Way, but I cannot take the steps for the people.

10. Other people have the right *not* to share my burden for my ministry.

11. I rejoice at the workers God has called to the harvest and refuse all envy and jealousy in my life. It is well with my soul.

It took John and Jan several years to learn to replace their mis-beliefs with truth. They learned to love each other and to see their work through the eyes of love. They are, at this writing, starting anew as volunteers with a large national Christian youth organization. They are also doing youth work in the church they attend. They are not indispensable anymore. They are part of a great team of workers who live for God and want to see His will brought into being in the world. They've joined forces with brothers and sisters across continents and oceans and have said "Yes" to *love*, removing the driving, striving misbeliefs of pride that they were once enslaved to.

Suppose your telephone rings at 3 a.m. for the third time this week and you hear the words, "You're the *only* one I can talk to," what will you do? Will you sigh with self-importance and relinquish another night's sleep to help this troubled person? Or will you speak the *truth* to yourself?

I am NOT a person's ONLY answer. I am NOT indispensable. I will help as I can and at reasonable hours. My family is important. I am important. This troubled person is important. You pray for wisdom and discernment and then you speak without hesitation: "I know that you're troubled and your trouble is important to me. Jesus is your only answer, as He is mine. I want to see you and work with you, but not now. Please call tomorrow and make an appointment to see me and we will work hard on your problem."

The Lord is demonstrating himself through you in the glory of love and truth. You are important, unique, special and beautiful, but thank God, none of us is indispensable.

More Misbeliefs Guaranteed To Make You Miserable

Now that you have read this far, you have more than likely developed some skill in identifying your misbeliefs and are doing something about them.

The first step, remember, is always *identifying* the misbelief. Second, you *argue* against it, and third, you *replace* it with the TRUTH. Say you're feeling frustrated, for example. You're tense and nervous and saying things like, "I wish I had more energy. I just can't seem to get through a day anymore without wearing out about halfway through."

Now, because you have become aware of your own self-talk and the role it plays in your life, you are paying special attention to your thoughts and words. You're listening carefully because you now know that your self-talk isn't always in complete sentences. Often it's an impression, feeling, or general mood due to a belief or misbelief.

You may express nonspecific discontent and not attach *words* to your feelings. You may say things like, "I wish I could stay in bed all day and not get up." (But listen further. *What* are you telling yourself?) "I just feel like a real nothing." (Locate your misbelief!) "Two of my closest friends are getting married. I'm not getting

174

married. I wish I were getting married." (Keep going. So far so good.) "I don't have what I want; therefore I must be a nothing." (Bull's-eye!) There's your misbelief.

The Attitudes That Accompany Misbeliefs

The above untruth is then implemented with other attitudes such as "Getting what I want is vital to my happiness. I must get what I want at all costs." You can recognize the slave-driving quality here: sure-fire misery.

Let's take a look at six popular misbeliefs and at the same time look at the accompanying misbelief behaviors and attitudes. If you believe you must get what you want in order to be happy, what kind of misbelief behavior will you develop to accompany it?

MISBELIEF #1	ACCOMPANYING ATTITUDES
I must get what I want in order to be happy. (I want it; therefore I should have it.)	It's terrible if I don't get what I want.
	My wants are the most important thing in the world.
	Doing without is intense suffering.
	If other people have what I want and I don't have it, it's unfair.
	I have to do all I can to get what I want.
	I'm happy when I have what I want.
	Other people must be as frustrated and unhappy as I am if they don't have what they want.
	Other people must want the same things I do; therefore, it's depressing to me to see people in want.
	If I don't have what I want, there must be something wrong with me as a Christian.
	If I don't have what I want, God must not hear my prayers.

The truth is none of the above.

175

Truth

- God loves me and always answers my prayers!
- The Bible says that the Lord will never leave me nor forsake me; therefore, I know that everything in my life is under His watchful eye!
- It's not terrible when my every whim isn't gratified!
- It's not terrible when my every need isn't met on my terms and time schedule!
- It may be uncomfortable or inconvenient to do without certain things, but I CAN DO IT!
- It is well with my soul! I will tell myself the truth! I can do without, I can be hassled and annoyed from time to time, but I can know in the recesses of my very being that through it all, I choose it to be well with my soul!
- I give others the right to be more successful than I, to have what I want!
- I set myself free from covetousness. I refuse to be a jealous person. It is well with my soul!
- I choose to love the Lord Jesus more than my own wants, and that's why I can give my wants to Him to bestow, bless, withhold or change.

Here are some additional misbeliefs, ideally tailored to add deep wounds and hurts to your life and keep them there.

MISBELIEF #2	ACCOMPANYING ATTITUDES
It's terrible to have hurt feelings.	Therefore, I must avoid situations and people who might hurt me.
	People who hurt me are bad.
	I'm less of a person when my feelings are hurt.
	Other people shouldn't have their feelings hurt, either.
	I must do everything to avoid hurting other people's feelings.
	People who hurt the feelings of my loved ones are bad.

MISBELIEF #2	ACCOMPANYING ATTITUDES
	I must make people treat me kindly and not hurt my feelings.
	I must always try to make others happy and never cause any trouble because someone might get hurt.
	I must try at all times to be "above it all." A Christian should never feel hurt.

See the nonsense? What incredible self-defeat! A person who is victimized by the above misbelief might also be like Carrie, in a previous chapter, enslaved to obligations and expectations. "If I don't do what's expected of me, I might disappoint so-and-so, and that would be terrible. She/he might say something bad to me and hurt my feelings. *I can't have my feelings hurt because that's terrible.* I had better take the safe road and try to please everybody." This way the confused person can affect a shallow "above-it-all nothing-bothers-me" posture. Francis Bacon said "Truth will sooner come out from error than from confusion." The Bible says Jesus heals both confusion *and* error.

The *truth* is, it's perfectly normal for the Christian to feel hurt once in a while. When your self-esteem is attacked, you may feel hurt or angry, depending upon the accompanying circumstances. The *truth* is, these reactions are okay because the *truth* is, you can handle it according to the Word of God and replace the phony self-talk with such statements as:

The Truth

- It is not unspiritual to have hurt feelings. I can have hurt feelings and still be a spiritual person.
- It is good for me to listen to my self-talk and hear the lies I tell myself in order to replace them with the truth. It is good for me to face the misbelief I have held that it is terrible to have hurt feelings. I stand against that lie now in the name of JESUS!

- I don't have to try to be above it all. I'm filled with the Holy Spirit and He is above it all. I choose to have mercy on myself, as God does.

- The Lord is my rock and my salvation. He is my defender and my shield. I have nothing whatever to fear. My body, my spirit, mind, and emotions are His.

- I give people the right to be hurtful and be hurt. I am nobody's savior. Jesus is Savior.

You can add many more statements of truth to this list. Take a separate sheet in your notebook and write as many true statements as you can to oppose this misbelief and the ones that follow.

MISBELIEF #3	ACCOMPANYING ATTITUDES
In order to be happy, I must be loved by everybody.	I must work hard to make everybody love me.
	I must flatter, manipulate and diligently endeavor to make certain I do just what people like.
	If people don't love me, I can't be happy.
	People who aren't loved by others must be very miserable.
	People who aren't loved by others must be failures.
	If people don't love me, I'm a failure.
	People owe it to me to love me.
	It's terrible to be unpopular.
	People who are famous, popular and adored by others are successful.
	If I am famous, popular and adored by others I will be successful.
	If nobody loves me, I might as well end it all. I'm useless.

MISBELIEF #4	ACCOMPANYING ATTITUDES
Things have to go right.	I have to defend everything I think is right.
	I must crusade for rightness in my home, at work, at church, in the neighborhood and everywhere else I go.

MISBELIEF #4	ACCOMPANYING ATTITUDES
	People shouldn't make mistakes.
	I must not make mistakes.
	If I make mistakes, I'm inept.
	When things go wrong, someone is to blame and they ought to be corrected.

MISBELIEF #5	ACCOMPANYING ATTITUDES
If it's worth doing, it's worth doing the BEST!	Doing a poor job of something is terrible and unforgivable.
	I can't forgive myself if I do poorly on something.
	I can't tolerate a poor job.
	Not getting the best grades, the best results, is a blot on a person's character.
	People who don't work hard or achieve success are lazy and inept.
	Lack of success is a sign of failure.
	Lack of success is a sign of not trying hard enough.
	If my children, friends, spouse don't agree with my demands for achievement, there's something wrong with them.
	If you can't give your very best to something, don't do it at all.
	Jesus expects us to do our best at all times.
	Jesus expects us to give our all; nothing less will do.
	Jesus is not pleased with us when we do a job poorly.

MISBELIEF #6	ACCOMPANYING ATTITUDES
I should always be and act happy in spite of all hardship or trouble that comes my way.	Feeling bad or upset is not being a good Christian.
	People will find out that I'm not a good Christian if they see I'm troubled or distressed.
	It would be terrible if people didn't think I'm a good Christian.
	I must be admired and looked up to, no matter what.
	I must maintain my perfect testimony in this dark and cruel world; otherwise God won't be pleased with me.

MISBELIEF #6	ACCOMPANYING ATTITUDES
I should always be and act happy in spite of all hardship or trouble that comes my way.	It's up to me to convert the world with my ever-strong and courageous attitudes and actions.
	There's something wrong with me if I don't receive trouble and hardship with a thankful heart.
	I should be *happy* when trouble comes my way.
	It's sinful to cry or feel sorry for myself. I must never let anyone know I do these things. They'll think less of me.
	Nobody must ever find out what a sinner I am. I must hide my feelings and "Put on a Happy Face" like the song says.

The foregoing six misbeliefs are somewhat related to one another in that as a result of your slavery to them, you can wind up hiding out in a hospital somewhere being terribly sick (avoidance behavior; the accompanying anxieties are just too much), or you can be depressed, frustrated, suicidal, or angry, in the throes of furiously flung assaults of doubt at God.

Words like, "I can't take this Christian way of life any longer! It's too hard! I just can't live up to what I'm supposed to be!"

Or, "Nobody loves me. If I stuck my head in the oven tonight and turned on the gas, nobody would even care. Why go on at all?"

Or, "What do you mean you didn't get the raise at work? What's the matter with you? Didn't you try hard enough?"

"I got a C on the exam. There must be something wrong with me."

These propagandizing habits need to be replaced with the *truth*. Truth is the unity in which Jesus Christ is the organizing principal and center. The smallest truth of everyday life is part and parcel of that one great *truth* which holds the universe together by the One who is *above* all, *through* all, and *in* all.

A Christian is not a person who is dominated by outside forces of the world, not one whose happiness or unhappiness depends upon situations, circumstances, or attending events. The Christian's happiness comes through his/her knowledge of Jesus and the power of God within. The indwelling Holy Spirit permeates every attitude, belief, dream, hope and thought. "I am complete in Him!" is his triumphant and *true* self-talk.

This doesn't mean you must never change an unpleasant situation! Please know that this book is not telling you to passively accept all suffering and pain without attempting to change it. When it is appropriate and within your power to remove the pain by changing the situation, *not* to do it would be destructive and downright silly. Example: A young man with a college degree in art takes a job as an insurance salesman even though there have been job openings in the field for which he qualified. He doesn't like the job he has and is unhappy and unsatisfied in it. In spite of this, he stays where he is while telling himself it's okay to suffer. Foolishness, right?

You don't become genuinely happy and fulfilled by some quirk of luck or accident. Everlasting joy is not a state of being that comes flying across the airwaves bringing with it peace and gladness just because things "go right," or somebody else decides you're a worthwhile person, or the right job just happens to fall into your lap.

During the years when World War II was raging in Europe, the small villages of Yugoslavia were hard hit with bombs, gun-fire, reprisals, and hardships of every kind. The Nazis dropped bombs from overhead, the Partisan army fired the guns, the Italians fired the guns, the Ustase army fired the guns, the Cetniks fired the guns—the villagers hardly knew which flag to wave when soldiers marched down their battleworn roads. But there was one family by the name of Kovac who clung to their faith in God even though it looked as though the whole world was going to pieces. Death and destruction were everywhere with no end in sight.

Jozeca Kovac was a young wife and mother who had made a commitment to Jesus with her whole heart, and she and her husband gave their lives to Him for better or worse. It certainly looked as though this war was the worst, even worse than the one preceding, World War I. One day Jozeca was thrown into jail with several other women. The following is a portion from the book about the Kovac family, *Of Whom the World Was Not Worthy*:

181

"The cells, which were hardly big enough for one person, held eight women in each. There were two pallets to sleep on and two blankets. There was a drain in the middle of the floor and one window near the ceiling with bars across it.

"'I shall not shed another tear,' she vowed, and she kept that vow for the next thirty days spent in that cell.

"They received their first meal the next afternoon. The guard threw it on the floor by the drain which also served as their toilet. The pot of gray liquid had fish scales floating in it.

"'Ah, stew!' exclaimed Jozeca. 'Come on, girls, let us eat.'

"But the smell was so pungent they could not lift the cup to the chin without wincing.

"'Rotten fish!' one of the girls wept. 'They are feeding us rotten fish!'

"'Do they call this food! This is food for the pigs!'

"'It is garbage!'

"Jozeca's eyes flashed. 'And we will get down on our knees and thank God for it!'

"Jozeca held the cup in front of her mouth and kissed it. 'Thank you, Lord,' she prayed, 'for this food which will keep us alive.' The others got on their knees also and they ate the stinking soup without another word."[1]

Later Jozeca prays and tells the girls that the Holy Book says if God's people will obey His commandments and follow His ways, He will pour out His blessings upon them. A thin, gray-haired woman winces angrily.

"What means this, *blessing*?" she asks incredulously.

Jozeca answers with assurance, "Why, to know *Him*," she says. "There is only one blessing—the blessing of knowing Him!"

Jozeca's joy did not depend on happy circumstances, did not depend upon the approval of others, did not depend upon pleasant

1. Marie Chapian, *Of Whom the World Was Not Worthy* (Minneapolis, MN: Bethany Fellowship, 1978).

surroundings, comfort, personal advantages, salubrious conditions or even answered prayer!

Happy is something you teach yourself to be.

You *teach* yourself to be happy no matter what circumstances, events or situations you face. You teach yourself to be contented because YOU have decided you are a worthwhile person. You know you are a worthwhile person because *God* says so! "For the Lord will not forsake his people; he will not abandon his heritage."[2] "The Lord is your keeper; the Lord is your shade on your right hand. The sun shall not smite you by day, nor the moon by night."[3]

> Fear not, for I have redeemed you; I have called you by name, you are mine. When you pass through the waters I will be with you; and through the rivers, they shall not overwhelm you; when you walk through fire you shall not be burned, and the flame shall not consume you.[4]

Who says you're worthwhile? *God* does! ("If God is for us, who is against us?" says Romans 8:31. If God is for you, don't YOU be against you.)

How do you "be against" you? Which of the following do you tell yourself the most? Be honest.

☐ I am dumb.	☐ Thank you, Lord, for giving me intelligence.
☐ I am unattractive.	☐ Thank you, Lord, for making me attractive.
☐ I can't—(whatever)	☐ I *can* with your help, Lord!
☐ Most people are happier than I.	☐ Thank you, Lord, for the happiness in my life.
☐ I'm poor.	☐ Thank you, Lord, for prospering me.
☐ People don't like me.	☐ Thank you, Lord, for making me likable.
☐ I have no talents.	☐ Thank you, Lord, for the talents you've given me!
☐ I'm miserable.	☐ Thank you, Lord, for the power to overcome.
☐ I'm lonely.	☐ Thank you, Lord, for being my faithful and dearest companion.

2. Psalm 94:14 (RSV).
3. Psalm 121:5, 6 (RSV).
4. Isaiah 43:1–2 (RSV).

Did you check more sentences on the left than on the right? Those sentences on the left are, for the most part, sheer hogwash. The sentences on the right are words of truth. Look at the sentences on the left and tell yourself, "Keep thy tongue from evil, and thy lips from speaking guile. Depart from evil, and do good; seek peace, and pursue it."[5]

Now, read out loud the list of *truths* on the right. Read them and rejoice. Jesus died on the cross to save you from deceit and false notions. He died to save you from the words in the left-hand column. You can add your own lies to that list. How many more have you been defaming yourself with?

The words you tell yourself have power over your life. If you tell yourself something often enough, eventually you'll believe it. Those little jokes you tell about how dumb or inept you are aren't jokes at all, they're more like curses. If you tell yourself enough times that you can't do anything right, you'll start believing it. Then, when something goes against your plans or you make a mistake, your previous lying self-talk becomes a conviction. You may say, "It figures that I'd do something stupid like that. I'm such a jerk."

Listen to the words you tell yourself. Are you building a tar baby? If you are, you can begin building castles and treasures in the kingdom of God by speaking the *truth*. Speak the promises of God in the Word of God. Speak these words to yourself *daily*!

[I] am more than a conqueror through him who loved [me]. For I am sure that neither death, nor life, nor angels, nor principalities, nor things present, nor things to come, nor powers, nor height, nor depth, nor anything else in all creation, will be able to separate [me] from the love of God in Christ Jesus [my] Lord.[6]

Now that you're really moving along with the truth, add some more to it, like this:

5. Psalm 34:13.
6. Romans 8:37–39 (RSV).

184

I am sure that neither lying self-talk nor vain lies about myself, nor attacks of the devil on my thoughts, nor my misbeliefs of the present, past or future, nor the ways of the world, nor positive thinking (which takes my mind away from GOD THINKING), nor any other ridiculous lie of the devil will be able to separate me from the love of God in Christ Jesus my Lord.

Remember, "A wholesome tongue is a tree of life: but perverseness therein is a breach in the Spirit."[7]

You're no dummy. You've come against the misbeliefs that have held you captive. Yours is now the tongue of the wise, and "the tongue of the wise is health."

Welcome home.

7. Proverbs 15:4.

185

What Must I Do to Be Miserable?

Or,

When the Truth Does Not Set Us Free

You can tell Esther is seriously disturbed from the moment she enters the waiting room. She huddles close to her tall, gaunt husband and stares across the row of comfortable chairs at the paintings on the wall. She wears the masklike expression every clinician comes to associate with either severe depression or schizophrenia.

Has Jesus not given a promise that holds true forever and all time, that the truth would have the power to set people free?

In the counseling room she speaks slowly and in a monotone voice. She looks at no one in particular and takes long pauses as she speaks.

Other Christian counselors and friends have told Esther that she has nothing to be depressed about. It's all in her head. They have told her she should be smiling and happy; after all, Jesus has given her His joy. They have advised her to pray more, praise more, give more and do more, and these well-intentioned words have only

186

served to depress her further. She is now plunged into a black hole of despair that nobody has been able to penetrate.

The advice the counselors and friends gave Esther was true enough, but it made her feel guilty and condemned. The truth didn't set her free. Why? What was wrong?

Throughout this first interview she exhibits confusion, disorientation and delusional thinking. The struggle for her happiness will be all-out war with the devil of lies. She is diagnosed as suffering acute severe depression, and she will be treated without medication. The therapeutic tool will be *truth*.

Many times people who think counseling is simple cause more guilt and anxiety than they resolve. Esther had been devastated by the counseling she received, even though the words were true enough.

Imagine you are the client in the following dialogue. You have gone to someone you respect seeking advice and counsel because you can't shake the depression you're experiencing.

You:	I've been feeling depressed lately. I can't seem to pick myself up. I don't know what's wrong with me.
Counselor:	Why are you feeling so bad?
You:	I don't know. I can't figure it out.
Counselor:	Is there some sin in your life you haven't confessed?
You:	I don't think so, but I'll gladly confess anything at all if you think I should.
Counselor:	Someone you haven't forgiven?
You:	I don't think so, but I'll gladly pray if you think I should.
Counselor:	We need to pray for the healing of your memories. (At this point you pray with the counselor.) (After praying) You know, friend, you have to realize you are a child of God. Shame on you for these feelings. Jesus died to take away sadness and gloom, and the Scriptures tell us to "rejoice in the Lord always."
You:	Yes, I know you're right. I feel so terrible about being depressed. I don't do much rejoicing.
Counselor:	You probably don't praise the Lord either! Do you praise the Lord every day?

You:	Oh, I guess I don't really. I mean, especially when I'm feeling depressed like this . . .
Counselor:	When a Christian is truly walking in the Spirit, the Word says he will experience life and peace! Your feelings of depression are in the flesh, not the spirit. You're not praising and you're not walking in the Spirit.
You:	I'm sure you're right. My wife (husband/friend) tells me the same thing. I'm told I should be an overcomer. But I'm really so depressed . . .
Counselor:	Just listen to the words of your mouth, will you? What you say is what you get, you know.
You:	What I say is what I get?
Counselor:	That's right. You *say* you're depressed and you'll *be* depressed.
You:	So I should say I'm *not* depressed?
Counselor:	The Word of God tells us that the power of life and death is in the tongue. Ask and you receive, you know.
You:	Okay, I'm not depressed. I'm not depressed.
Counselor:	That's better. Now just rejoice in the Lord. Praise the Lord and you'll be over that depression in no time.

How would you feel after this counseling session? Probably very frustrated, and perhaps more guilty and depressed than ever.

Why did the truth not set you free?

Let's examine this dialogue to see what was going on in this counselor's mind. We would be safe to say he believed:

1. Counseling is very simple once you've become a Christian. All you have to do is know some scripture verses and some popular current teachings.

2. There is no need to listen to people since feeling bad and having unsolved problems is always a result of sin and failure to apply the Word of God.

3. Knowing scripture verses is all a counselor needs to help a person who is having problems. If a troubled person doesn't want to hear the truth, it's just too bad.

Not everything this counselor believes is false. It *is* true that the Word of God heals and cleanses ("Now ye are clean through the word which I have spoken unto you"[1]), and it *is* true that some problems are the result of sin and failure to apply the Word of God. Why, then, did this counselor's words not zero into the sting of depression and help to remove it?

Esther was told to go home and quit being upset because being so upset was sinful and self-centered. Her friends told her she was selfish to feel so depressed, and if she repented of her selfishness the Lord would cleanse her of her sins and she'd feel better again. She was not offered any means of understanding her own dynamics or any *procedures* for change. She heard only the stern demands to do what she couldn't do.

Esther was supposed to just stop feeling bad and start loving the Lord the way she ought to; after all, He had done so much for her, why wasn't she more thankful? The more times she heard those words, the more deeply she agonized over her failures and mistakes. She began to believe that she was worthless and inadequate, that maybe she wasn't even a Christian.

Sometimes the troubled person, such as Esther, will be accused of having demons. We know of one woman who was accused of being possessed with a "demon of national pride." She was from a foreign country and her strong ties to her homeland apparently displeased her accusers. Another woman explained how she was accused of demon possession. "I was told my home had a spirit of art. I was shocked to think that a demon of art lived in my house! So I burned all my paintings and gave away my collection of antique books and magazines. I didn't want to be out of the Lord's will and so I stripped the place of all the art. I tossed out thousands of dollars of precious art."

The help that doesn't help and the truth that doesn't set people free can be due to:

1. Counselors or helpers who haven't any real or genuine love for people who are hurting.

1. John 15:3.

2. Failure to hear what the troubled person is really saying, and instead of listening for leads into the problems, cutting them off.

3. Not bothering to learn anything about the troubled person.

4. Using the Word of God as a club to beat them with the truth.

5. Knowing all the answers and being ready with solutions at all times.

6. The mistaken thought that the counselor is a better and more worthy person than the disturbed person.

Jesus can meet every problem a human being can have, but it takes wisdom and discernment on the part of the counselor to hear how He wants each person handled. The counselor should pray for the spiritual gifts of knowledge and discernment and the wisdom to use them effectively. Helping people's emotions to be healthy is not like handing out the same prescription for every cold and sore throat. Not everyone suffers anxiety or depression alike or for the same reasons.

There are no pat answers to emotional suffering.

There are many theories, and each theorist thinks his is the truth. The cause of trouble, according to some theories of psychopathology, is unconscious conflict, caused in its turn, by childhood interactions and events. Closely related to this is the notion that memories are the causes of current difficulties and if the memories are healed, all will be well.

Still other theories locate the causes of all behavior difficulties in the genes, offering the dubious consolation that such things can be bred out of future generations, provided we will all mate as the scientists plan for us to; or perhaps have our genetic material altered.

Other scientists insist that chemical imbalance underlies all unwanted emotion, proposing that psychopharmacologists develop elixirs, tablets and capsules which, when ingested, will produce an anxiety and depression-free world.

Then there are the religious folk who insist emotional trouble is always due to unrepented sin and lack of faith. Other religious people may locate the cause in the spirit, under the assumption that infestation by evil spirits is inevitable, especially in cases they do not understand such as dyslogic syndrome and schizophrenia. In actuality, there may be some truth in all these theories, but none of them in themselves is sufficient explanation and cure for all disordered behavior.

The fact that improvement occasionally follows the use of these treatment methods does not mean that each by itself is "the answer."

God desires to work wholeness through measures such as prayer, laying-on of hands, anointing with oil, deliverance, counseling, diet, medication, work, play, fresh air, exercise, friends, human love and also, at times, a psychotherapeutic relationship. (When the Lord has chosen to produce desired effects through counseling, it is not an alternative to "letting God do it," but rather the means He has determined to use in the particular case.)

Esther learned how to listen to the words and thoughts in her mind. She listened to the words she was telling herself which perpetuated her negative feelings.

"I just hate getting up in the mornings," she explained in the lethargic tone of voice she had adopted. "Mornings are just rotten. I hate facing the house, the kids and the mess. I hate getting out of bed. But I hate going to bed, too. I can't sleep. I wake up a thousand times a night. I never feel rested. I just hate everything. I don't see a thing good in anything."

"Esther, when you wake up in the morning and sit on the edge of the bed, what are your first *thoughts?*"

"I don't know if I think anything. I *just feel* rotten. I feel like I wish I could just die." She pauses, stares at the lamp on the desk, then says, "I tell myself I can't handle it—I can't handle any of it."

Another long pause. She pushes her mouth downward into a pout. "Nothing I do is right. That's what I tell myself."

Esther believed God made impossible demands on her, life made impossible demands of her. She thought she couldn't meet up with expectations made of her and now she lacked the strength to try to live up to her own expectations. She wasn't far from the truth. It was all just too much.

She had made her life the way it was. She dreamed of being married, of being the perfect wife. She dreamed of the day when she would have sweet little children around, all cute, lovable, and subservient. She dreamed of dressing them up in adorable clothes and having them near her all day for company; she'd just love motherhood. She wanted to be the *best* wife, the *best* mother, and the *best* Christian there could possibly be.

Her husband had certain expectations, too. He expected Esther to keep a neat house; teach the children obedience, manners, and respect, while loving it; have delicious meals ready when he came home from work; keep herself neat and attractive; be devoted and appreciative of him; consider his wants vitally important and be dependent upon him for her rewards in life.

The children demanded she be there 100% of the time to feed, diaper, amuse, clothe, care for and delight in them. She felt guilty that she didn't enjoy her noisy children and cluttered house more than she did and couldn't understand why she lost her temper during the day so often.

She compared herself with her Christian friends who seemed on top of things. She compared herself with the women on the TV commercials whose floors glistened merrily after a quick flick of the mop and whose children smelled beautiful, looked beautiful, and acted beautiful. She was familiar with the TV programs where the little wife always seemed to have it all together. She looked at herself and thought, "I dreamed of married life being like heaven and it turned out to be like purgatory."

Expectations too great to meet, demands too impossible to achieve, where was God in all this?

Her church was active with some program going for every day of the week. Esther started out by attending the Women's Wednesday morning Bible study plus the Sunday morning church service. Gradually, she joined the Missionary Society which met on Fridays, the intercessory prayer group which met Tuesday mornings, and she volunteered to help in the nursery for the Sunday night services. She attended the Sunday School Workers' Brunches once a month.

People liked her and appreciated her eagerness to help. She thought they expected her to be energetic, giving, concerned, and involved at all times. "The world is watching you," her pastor expounded from the pulpit on Sunday morning. "Always bear in mind that the world has got its eye on the Christian! It's up to you to be a good witness!"

A good witness, a good wife, a good mother, a good Christian, a good person, a good cook, a good church worker—demands, pressures, expectations! Esther forged ahead, struggling, trying, laboring to be "good," the "best," until she failed so often and felt so guilty, she started feeling depressed.

Then came the demands to rise above her depressed feelings. "You're supposed to be an overcomer!" "Depression is sin!" "But you ought to be victorious!"

Esther's ideas of the perfect wife, mother, and Christian flew out of her grasp like paper streamers in the wind. With nothing to replace these false ideals, she felt worthless, defeated, devoid of a dream, useless, and sinful.

But the Truth Does Set Us Free!

A frequent cause of disordered behavior is a person's failure to examine his/her beliefs (attitudes, ideas, thoughts, self-talk) and the concomitant tendency not to question them, though they be painful, cruel, and UNtrue. Locating and identifying pain-causing fabrications plus learning the factual reality-based *truth* was the therapeutic "miracle" which began Esther's dramatic recovery.

Let's repeat the Three-Point Misbelief Therapy Outline:

1. Locate and identify the misbelief in your thinking and self-talk.

(Esther's misbelief, at least in part, was: "I'm a failure at life because I'm not the wife or mother I thought I'd be and being married isn't what it's cracked up to be at all.")

2. Argue against the misbelief.

("I'm not a failure just because I didn't meet expectations that were unrealistic in the first place. Marriage may not be what I dreamed it would be, that's true, but there are some things about it that aren't all that bad.")

3. Replace the misbelief with the TRUTH.

("In spite of the unpleasantness, disappointments and daily trials I experience, I *can* carry on. The demands that I be joyful and energetic at all times are unrealistic, and Jesus died on the cross so I can be unashamed to be real. I'm not a failure because I feel bad at times. I am a born-again child of God with a Savior who saves me from my own demands and expectations of myself and others.")

"I can change the situations in my life that need changing without fearing I'm making a mistake. I am no longer intimidated by the demands of others."

"Furthermore," Esther told herself, "I *can* get through unpleasant feelings and admit that I occasionally have them even though I have believed the fable that other people are happy all the time. I *can* be content even if things aren't as I would like them to be. I *can* get through discomfort because *I can do all things through Christ which strengtheneth me*."[2]

2. Philippians 4:13.

Jesus taught that the *truth* has freeing power. God looks for and wants *truth* to be present in our innermost being. "Behold, thou desirest truth in the inward parts: and in the hidden part thou shalt make me to know wisdom"[3] is our prayer.

Whether we are the ones suffering or whether we are counseling someone else who is suffering, our task is to communicate the *truth* which frees the inward parts, our souls, where our emotions live.

Esther made rapid improvements when she realized many of her misbeliefs. She taught herself to replace lies with the truth in her life. She taught herself to have mercy on herself, also. She taught herself to discuss her feelings with her husband and to let him know if his demands of her were unrealistic.

Living up to others' expectations will wear down the best of us and cause us to lose our own sense of self-worth to the all-prevailing menace of others-worth.

It's through the power of truth we find our personhood, making it the very foundation of our lives. Telling ourselves the truth sets us free to be the dynamic, loving, altogether whole people God meant us to be.

As a Christian, that same spirit that raised Christ from the dead dwells in you. You're His child and you are never alone as you spend the rest of your life, and indeed all of eternity, telling yourself the truth.

If this book has helped you, you will want to read *Teaching Your Children to Tell Themselves the Truth*, by the same authors. It provides parents with a simple, easy-to-follow plan to help their children learn the truth and use it to shape their lives.

3. Psalm 51:6.

Study Guide

How to Use This Study Guide

We have prepared this study guide to stimulate your thinking and increase your ability to remember and apply the principles of *Telling Yourself the Truth*. Using the study guide will help you put Misbelief Therapy into actual practice immediately. If you will honestly identify, challenge, and replace your misbeliefs as we have outlined, you will obtain dramatic and positive results in your feelings and actions.

This study guide is written for group participation as well as individual use. Read a chapter in the book, and then work on the corresponding material in the study guide. Refer to the book and restudy sections as the need arises. As you work, be sure to focus on your own true feelings and beliefs.

A group study program can be developed by having class members discuss the questions in the study guide each week before working on them and then working on the lesson at home before the next meeting. The group then discusses each question from a personal experience standpoint, each member sharing the work God is doing in his or her own life.

We are praying continually for you who read the book and use the study guide that you will experience great and joyous victories through telling yourself the truth, finding a fulfilled and rich life in Jesus Christ, who loves you.

Marie Chapian
William Backus

CHAPTER ONE

What Is a Misbelief?

1. List the misbeliefs you have in common with Jerry:

2. Solely on the basis of the material in the text, which one of the two great thinkers about truth appeals most to you: Descartes or Marcus Aurelius? Why?

3. List three basic steps to becoming the happy person you were meant to be:

4. Take step one for yourself now, and jot down a few of your own most commonly troublesome misbeliefs.

5. Are all of our irrational beliefs in verbal form? Explain.

6. Why is Freudian philosophy a good thing to leave behind if you want to overcome your present misbelief?

7. What is the cause of most of our current emotions or feelings?

8. What is the difference between *unbelief* and a *misbelief*?

9. God wills that we suffer depression at times and sends us many other persistent painful emotions. True or false? Give reasons for your answer.

10. It doesn't matter what a person believes as long as he or she is totally sincere. True or false? Give reasons for your answer.

CHAPTER TWO

Do We Really Want to Be Happy?

1. Give one reason from the text why Freudian psychoanalytic theory is no longer as widely accepted among psychologists and psychiatrists as it once was.

2. Why can you expect Misbelief Therapy to work for you even if nothing else has?

3. "I can't change the way I am!" is an especially crippling misbelief. Why?

4. What is the difference between the therapies of medicine and surgery and misbelief therapy insofar as the involvement of the patient is concerned?

5. List some reasons why it may be important to examine your early years:

6. Fill in the blanks: Change a man's beliefs and you will change his _____ and _____ .

7. What does the state of your biochemistry have to do with your feelings?

8. Name some things that can alter the state of your biochemistry and thus change your feelings:

9. Can thoughts affect your brain chemistry? Can brain chemistry affect your thinking and feeling?

10. List some terms other psychologists have used for the process of changing people's misbeliefs in order to improve feelings:

CHAPTER THREE

Misbelief in Self-Talk

1. Define self-talk:

2. Do you think it is harmless to put yourself down repeatedly? Why or why not?

3. If you tell somebody "You can't do anything right" enough times, eventually the person will . . .

4. Married people envy _____ .
   Single people envy _____ .

5. The basic misbelief of both above groups is, "I'm unhappy and someone else is _____ ."

6. Write out what the apostle Paul learned about this matter in Philippians 4:11.

7. Why are untrue self-statements like a tar baby?

8. Write some of the destructive thoughts that are typically generated in us by demonic lying:

9. Now write three truths, at least, that can counter the misbeliefs in your answer to number 8:

10. Keep thy tongue from _____ , and thy _____ from _____ (Ps. 34:13).

11. The above verse applies not only to speaking evil of other people or things but of speaking evil and guile against:

12. Psalm 34:14 reads, "Depart from evil and do good; seek peace, and pursue it." How can you do this regarding yourself? (Give at least two ways.)

CHAPTER FOUR

Misbelief in Depression

1. Write down three or four phrases in Scripture that describe depressed feelings. For example, Psalm 42 contains a descriptive phrase. Read through the Psalms and find more such phrases:

2. List at least three events that may provoke or precipitate depression:

3. Name the three areas of devaluation in depressive self-talk:

   a.

   b.

   c.

4. Give some typical examples of self-devaluing statements made by depressed people:

5. List some typical examples of situation-devaluing statements made by depressed people:

6. List some typical examples of future-devaluing self-talk statements:

7. Tell what it is that gives your life meaning.

8. Give an example of a mistaken way to combat depression.

9. True or false: "You should never admit that you feel sad or depressed." Give reasons for your answer.

10. Tell what is wrong with the misbelief that some things or people are so vital to us that we cannot go on after losing them.

CHAPTER FIVE

Misbelief in Anger

1. True or false: "All anger is bad." Give scriptural support for your answer.

2. Why can't you simply ignore anger in yourself until it goes away?

3. Tell why the following misbeliefs are false:

   a. "I have the right to *demand* that my husband (or) wife be a good husband (or) wife."

   b. "Because I am nice to others, they are *supposed* to be nice to me."

   c. "People ought to do the good things I want them to do *because* I want them to."

4. When I get upset over someone else's behavior, I am upsetting myself. The other person is not upsetting me. Explain why this is so.

5. Anger always means to yell and throw things. True or false? Tell why.

6. Why are statements like "I can't stand it any longer," "It's unendurable," "Life is awful, miserable," "Things are terrible; it's the absolute end of the world" nearly always false?

7. Define anger:

8. Tell what is wrong with the belief "I can't help it if I hold a grudge for a long time."

9. Discuss the moral distinction between the brief emotion of anger and prolonged anger or bitterness. (Refer to Ephesians 4:16 and James 1:19–20.)

10. List some physical illnesses that may be caused or aggravated by sustained anger:

11. Give some reasons why this statement is false: "There is nothing you can do about it when someone is angry with you."

CHAPTER SIX

Misbelief in Anxiety

1. Give a definition of anxiety:

2. Tell in simple words what is meant by "overestimation of the probability of a disaster."

3. What did Suzie's mother do to *teach* Suzie to be anxious?

4. Show from Suzie's case how one can continue to teach oneself to be and remain anxious.

5. What is meant by the term "awfulizing"?

6. List some of the misbeliefs we often have about other people that make and keep us anxious:

7. What is the central theme running through the misbeliefs that produce anxiety?

8. What are the misbeliefs of the acrophobic person?

9. List the misbeliefs of the zoophobic and the claustrophobic persons:

10. Write some truths that argue and counter the misbeliefs you listed in items 6–9:

11. What effect will avoidance behavior have on anxiety?

12. What can you tell yourself to help you overcome avoidance behavior?

CHAPTER SEVEN

Misbelief in Lack of Self-Control

1. Write a thing you really *need* and three things you *want* very much but do not literally *need*. (You can include things you already possess among the items on your lists.)

2. Can you explain why people who have a serious problem with self-control frequently manifest anger toward God?

3. Show how the public media encourage poor self-control.

4. What is false about this misbelief? "You cannot control your strong desires, since they are 'needs' and you *have* to have them fulfilled."

5. True or false: "You should never have to endure frustration or discomfort." Explain.

6. How do parents teach children to yell and demand immediate fulfillment and instant gratification?

7. What is the "Once-Fail-Always-Fail Misbelief"?

8. What is the "I Owe Myself a Little Misbelief"?

9. We are responsible for our choices. Can you think of ways you have tried to deny this truth?

10. Can you explain how a person might plan a program of self-reward to overcome a self-control problem? Work with an example of your own choosing.

11. What are "triggers" in connection with self-control problems? Give some examples:

CHAPTER EIGHT

Misbelief in Self-Hate

1. Arnie had a prevalent misbelief in his life. It made him miserable. What was it?

2. Examine yourself for a moment. At what points in your own life do you misbelieve that you *must* meet the expectations of other people?

3. True or false: The approval of other people is vital to being happy. Tell why or why not.

4. What two important truths does Scripture teach us about our self-worth?

5. True or false: A self-debaser flatters others to get their approval.

6. Name three additional behaviors that the self-debaser exhibits:

   a.

   b.

   c.

7. List the misbeliefs of the self-debaser:

8. After looking over Elaine's misbeliefs, determine how many of these exist in your own life:

9. Now tell yourself the truth regarding these misbeliefs. Write your personal "truth" statements:

10. Why is it godly to love yourself? Give scriptural support to your answers.

11. Much of our social custom teaches us to manipulate for acceptance and approval. Godly motives are higher. What are some of these motives? Complete the following:

I will _____ demand or insist you care about me.

I will _____ strive to earn your approval or affection or friendship.

I care about _____ and I also care about _____.

The approval of _____ is more important than the approval of _____.

CHAPTER NINE

Misbelief in Fear of Change

1. Tell why the following misbelief is false: "I am the way I am. I'll never change."

2. Nobody forces you to sin. You do it all by your own choosing. Nobody else makes you unhappy either. You make yourself unhappy. How do you make yourself unhappy?

3. True or false: The fault of the unsatisfactory conditions or circumstances in your life is outside of your own control.

4. Complete: "I am responsible for _____ feelings and actions." Now say it out loud five times.

5. Now list some of your misbeliefs that held you bound to others, making them responsible for your feelings. (Example: "So-and-so makes me nervous.")

6. For the most part, you *learned* how to think, feel, and act the way you do. Therefore, you can unlearn it.

7. Give biblical examples to prove that it is not necessary to live in perfect circumstances to be happy.

8. Argue these misbeliefs with the truth:

MISBELIEF	TRUTH
You make me angry!	(ex: I make myself angry.)
Nobody loves me and that's why I'm sad and miserable.	
My job depresses me.	
Life is unfair.	

9. There are times to alter your circumstances if they are negative and harmful to your well-being and happiness. Some ways to change are (check appropriate answer):

____ Ask other people to change behaviors that create problems for you.

____ Scream violently when your peace is disturbed.

____ Get sick so others will (at last) appreciate you.

____ Punch your fist through the wall to prove who's boss.

____ Remove yourself calmly from the disagreeable situation.

10. Jesus did not always accept and remain in every negative circumstance he encountered. Read John 10:31–42 and write His choice of behavior and your reactions.

11. Name three people in the Bible who chose to change *themselves* rather than stay the same:

CHAPTER TEN

Misbelief in Never Taking a Chance

1. Why is this statement false? "No matter what, my feelings shouldn't get hurt."

2. Why is this statement true? "It's okay to make a wrong decision sometimes."

3. Name three of Roland's misbeliefs and tell why they are misbeliefs:

4. Why does a person actually enjoy hearing about other people's tragedies and losses?

5. "To be rejected would be terrible" is a misbelief. Tell why.

6. God took a great risk when He created man with a free will. To Him the risk was worth it, even though man uses his will to rebel against God. God has taken many risks with man. Can you show examples?

7. How does God's willingness to take risks affect your life?

8. Is this statement true? Faith itself is a risk. Give three reasons for your answer:

9. Telling yourself the truth teaches that you can't lead a happy, peaceful life without risks. Explain.

10. Name some behaviors you avoid because they seem to you to be too risky (Example: Asking for a raise or telling someone you care for them):

11. Locate your negative self-talk regarding the behaviors and argue these words with the truth. Examples:

NEGATIVE SELF-TALK	TRUTH
"I don't dare ask for a raise. I might get turned down. That would be terrible."	"It's okay if I'm turned down for a raise, even though I really want it."

CHAPTER ELEVEN

Misbelief in Our Relationships with Others

1. True or false: Other people ought to live up to your expectations. (Explain.)

2. There are only two basic obligations we have as human beings. What are they?

3. False obligation says, "I must do such-and-such because it's expected of me." What does the obligation of love say?

4. The words "I ought" are preludes to feelings of guilt. Why?

5. Your expectations hurt you as well as others. When you demand that others fulfill your expectations, you make yourself a target for defeat. Here are some examples of non-biblical, non-spiritual demands for expectations along with their results when unmet:

EXPECTATION	RESULTS IF NOT MET
Husbands are supposed to eat the food wives prepare for them without complaining.	Feeling hurt, unloved, rejected.
Children should show interest in the piano when parents sacrifice for their lessons.	Feeling angry, unappreciated, frustrated.
(Add your own:)	

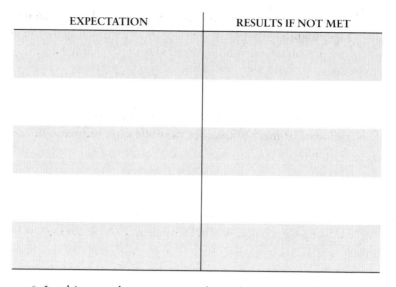

EXPECTATION	RESULTS IF NOT MET

6. Looking at what you wrote above, how can you change your self-talk by telling yourself the TRUTH? Use the space below to answer. Example:

   TRUTH: I don't have to have cooperation and approval to feel good about myself or to know that what I'm doing is okay.

7. List here the demands and expectations you've put upon others that you would now like to be free of:

8. Describe manipulation:

9. Argue the following manipulative statement with a statement of loving truth: "I've been home all day alone and nobody called me or came to see me, not even you, my very own son . . ."

10. What are some resulting emotions when we are manipulated by guilt?

11. Conversely, what are the resulting emotions of loving truth?

12. When is the truth not loving but a manipulative tool?
    Example:
    "I don't want to hurt your feelings, but I just feel that I ought to tell you in sincere Christian love that you are a big show-off, and truthfully speaking, you've got a big mouth, and besides that, you've made a big mess of things."

13. A key to telling the truth is: You must not accuse. What are some other rules for telling the truth?

    a.

    b.

    c.

14. "I have been crucified with _____; it is no longer I who live, but _____ who lives in me" (Gal. 2:20).

CHAPTER TWELVE

Misbelief in Being Indispensable

1. The Bible gives us an example of the overworked man of God in the experience of Moses (Ex. 18:1–26). According to Jethro, his father-in-law, why wasn't Moses Mr. Indispensable?

2. "You will surely _____ , both _____ and these _____ who are with you, for the task is _____ for you; you cannot _____ _____ ."

3. Give three examples of good when it is not so good.
   a.

    b.

    c.

4. Name five misbeliefs related to the idea that we are indispensable.

    a.

    b.

    c.

    d.

    e.

5. The following statement is true. Why? "It is an honor to be used of God, but I realize I am not responsible for providing the answers and solutions to everyone's problems."

6. Is this statement true? "Other people have the right *not* to particularly care about me and my needs." Explain.

7. Give three examples of pride as a motive for helping people:

   a.

   b.

   c.

8. What might the self-talk be for your above answers?

9. Argue these words with the TRUTH.

10. In your own words, why do you think it is important for you to understand why nobody is indispensable?

CHAPTER THIRTEEN

More Misbeliefs Guaranteed
to Make You Miserable

1. The first step in helping yourself overcome a problem is to locate and identify the accompanying _____ .

2. The second step is to _____ against it.

3. The third step is to _____ it with the TRUTH.

4. Suppose you are feeling frustrated. You're tense and nervous. Your self-talk goes like this: "I wish I had more energy. I just can't seem to get through a day anymore without wearing out about halfway through it." Locate two misbeliefs in such self-talk:

   a.

   b.

5. Starting on page 175 there is a list of misbeliefs and attitudes that accompany them. In the following space, write which ones might pertain to YOU.

MISBELIEF	ACCOMPANYING ATTITUDE

6. Now write the TRUTH regarding the above. For example, if you wrote "I must get what I want" as a misbelief, and the accompanying attitude is "Doing without is terrible!" argue this misbelief with the TRUTH:

7. Argue and replace the words in this misbelief with the TRUTH: "I should pretend to be happy and on top of the world even if I'm hurting and sad."

8. Is the following statement true? Why or why not? "A Christian is not a person who is dominated by outside forces of the world, and is not one whose happiness or unhappiness depends upon situations, circumstances, or attending events."

9. Jozeca Kovac, the heroine in the book *Of Whom the World Was Not Worthy*,[1] was thrown into jail in Yugoslavia and given food

---

1. Marie Chapian, *Of Whom the World Was Not Worthy* (Minneapolis: Bethany House Publishers, 1978).

to eat that was comparable to garbage. Yet she wholeheartedly thanked God for her blessings. How was this possible?

10. Jozeca Kovac demonstrates to us the truth that happy is something you _____ yourself to be.

11. Write ten statements about *yourself* beginning with the words "Thank you, Lord, for . . ." (Example: Thank you, Lord, for making me an intelligent person who can read and understand *Telling Yourself the Truth*.)

CHAPTER FOURTEEN

What Must I Do to Be Miserable?

Or, When the Truth Does Not Set Us Free

This chapter talks about using the truth with wisdom and compassion. Sometimes we can do harm by causing those we are trying to help to feel guilty and anxious with our well-meaning words. Some counselors, in an attempt to give someone the help he or she needs, will actually devastate the person.

1. Read the dialogue on pages 187–188. How many seemingly good, but in this case, non-helpful answers, is this counselor using? Write your answers here:

   a.

   b.

   c.

   d.

   e.

   f.

   g.

2. Why did this counselor fail to help the hurting person?

3. The help that doesn't help and the truth that doesn't set people free can be due to (give at least six answers and explain why):

4. Name ten measures through which God works to bring wholeness in a person's life:

5. Write ten personal statements beginning with the words "I can carry on in spite of . . ."

6. Psalm 51:6 reads, "Behold, thou desirest _____ in the inward parts: and in the hidden part thou shalt make me to know _____ ."

7. Whether we are the ones suffering or whether we are counseling someone else who is suffering, our task is to communicate the TRUTH, which frees the inward parts, our souls, where our emotions live. In your own words, why does telling yourself the truth set you free?

William Backus founded the Center for Christian Psychological Services, was a licensed consulting psychologist, and an ordained minister of the gospel. Dr. Backus did follow-up studies of his clients that showed a 95 percent improvement rate compared to a 67 percent success rate for other methods of therapy. He claimed that the difference was the truth of God as revealed in His Word. Dr. Backus died in June 2005.

Marie Chapian, PhD, has been teaching and writing inspirational books to empower Christians in their walk with God for over 20 years, with more than 30 books translated into 15 languages, including Chinese and Arabic. Her Christian writings have earned the Gold Medallion and the Cornerstone Book of the Year awards, among others. Her books include the A HEART FOR GOD devotional series and *Free to Be Thin*. She holds a doctorate in counseling and a Master of Fine Arts degree in creative writing, is heard and seen on radio and TV, and travels widely as a conference speaker. Visit Marie at www.mariechapian.com.

More From
Dr. William Backus

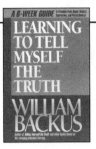

Put What You've Read Into Action

Based on the bestselling book *Telling Yourself the Truth*, this stand-alone workbook provides you with the tools you need to be free from the tyranny of emotional difficulties. Through self-evaluation, growth exercises, and spiritual discipleship, you will identify your own misbeliefs and replace them with the truth, leading to a life of true happiness.

Learning to Tell Myself the Truth

BAKER PUBLISHING GROUP